Stained Glass APPLIQUÉ

The SIMPLE FUSED WAY

Brenda
Brayfield
&
Lise
Merchant

*Enjoy the beauty of
stained glass quilts!
Brenda Brayfield*

Located in Paducah, Kentucky, the American Quilter's Society (AQS) is dedicated to promoting the accomplishments of today's quilters. Through its publications and events, AQS strives to honor today's quiltmakers and their work and to inspire future creativity and innovation in quiltmaking.

EDITOR: TONI TOOMEY
GRAPHIC DESIGN: AMY CHASE
COVER DESIGN: MICHAEL BUCKINGHAM
QUILT PHOTOS: CHARLES R. LYNCH
HOW-TO PHOTOS: BARBARA ST. HILAIRE

Library of Congress Cataloging-in-Publication Data

Brayfield, Brenda.
    Stained glass appliqué : the simple fused way / by Brenda Brayfield and Lise Merchant
        p. cm.
    ISBN 1-57432-868-9
    1. Appliqué--Patterns. 2. Quilting. 3. Patchwork. 4. Fusible materials in sewing.
I. Merchant, Lise. II. Title.

    TT779.B747 2004
    746.46'041--dc22

                        2004020292

Additional copies of this book may be ordered from the American Quilter's Society, PO Box 3290, Paducah, KY 42002-3290, or online at www.AmericanQuilter.com.

Dedications

This book is dedicated to my mother, Maureen Clough, a constant source of love and laughter. Mom, thoughts of you always bring a smile. To my husband, Roger, who continues to make everything possible. And to my wonderful children and grandchildren, the projects I'm the proudest of.

— Brenda Brayfield

I dedicate this book to my husband, Philip, for his love, devotion, and encouragement in everything I do. And to my sons, James, William, and Andrew, for their love and support.

— Lise Merchant

Acknowledgments

My heartfelt thanks and gratitude to my friend and co-author, Lise Merchant. Thank you for your willingness to embrace a new technique; your eagerness to undertake a new adventure; your artistic skill and creative flair; and for your enthusiasm and sense of humor. Thanks, Lise, it's a pleasure to work with you.

— Brenda Brayfield

My sincere thanks to Brenda Brayfield for inviting me to join her in this new adventure. Your friendship, trust, and unruffled demeanor mean a lot to me. It has been an exciting journey and a time of self-discovery and creative growth. Thank you, Brenda, for a fulfilling and rewarding experience.

To my mother, Marie Vadnais, who taught me the love of sewing at a very young age, and to my father, Gerard Champoux, and my sisters, France, Lucie, and Renee, for your faith and enthusiasm.

To my friend Lynn Blaikie for her encouragement and support.

To my friend and advisor, Dawn Bouquot, for introducing me to stained glass quilts.

— Lise Merchant

Contents

Introduction

Stained glass appliqué done the simple fused way is an easy, step-by-step technique that does not involve bias tape or glue, but it does guarantee spectacular results, even for the newest quilter. If you can trace and cut a smooth line, you can create gorgeous stained glass quilts.

"Necessity is the mother of invention" accurately describes how this technique came into being. In the autumn of 1997, I committed to teach a stained glass quilting class. My first effort left a lot to be desired. I was running out of time, the class was fast approaching, and I did not have time to perfect the technique described in the pattern. So I developed my own. The technique was an instant success with my students, and I have been perfecting it since then. New quilting products, such as the Mini Iron™ and quilt basting spray, have made the technique so much easier and better than when I started.

This book is a combination of my technical know-how and the artistic talent of Lise Merchant, a gifted stained glass artist from Whitehorse, Yukon. Upon the advice of an experienced quilter and friend, Lise decided to combine her love of sewing with her stained glass designs. She discovered her two passions were a natural blend.

We are very excited about this book and are delighted to be able to share our ideas and designs with you. The joy of recreating stained glass in fabric will soon be yours – enjoy its beauty!

Getting Started

Tools and Materials

All of the items needed to make the projects should be readily available from your local quilt shop or stationery store.

Your basic quiltmaking supplies should include a rotary cutter, a cutting mat large enough to accommodate the folded fabric width, and a 6" x 24" clear acrylic ruler.

For Stained Glass Appliqué

Starch. Starching the leading fabric before cutting will produce a smoother, cleaner cutting edge. We prefer liquid starch to the aerosol can. Mix ¼ cup starch with ¾ cup water in a spray bottle. Spray and press on the wrong side of the fabric. Spray moderately. Heavy spraying will prevent the transfer web from fusing properly. It is not necessary to starch the windowpane fabrics.

Tracing paper. Use semi-transparent paper in a size large enough to accommodate the pattern. Our favorite is 40 lb. white Kraft Paper purchased from an art supply store. It is more durable than tracing paper but transparent enough to see through.

Mechanical pencil. A mechanical pencil produces a fine, consistent line.

Permanent marker. Use an ultra-fine point to trace the design onto fusible transfer web.

Poster board. Securing the pattern to poster board makes tracing much easier because you rotate the design as you trace.

Low-tack tape. Use easily removable tape to secure the tracing paper to the book.

Fusible transfer web. Regular weight Wonder-Under® was used for all the projects in this book.

Sewing awl. Use a sewing awl or a stiletto to help nudge small fabric pieces into place.

Embroidery scissors. Good quality, small, sharp-to-the-tip scissors are essential to guarantee smooth, clean edges.

Freezer paper. Use freezer paper for the windowpane templates.

Highlighter. Use a colored highlighter to outline the edge of the windowpane templates.

Post-It® Flags. Use the ½" x 1¾" flags to secure the leading to the design pattern during fusing process.

Mini Iron™. This little tool is ideal for fusing the fabric pieces to the web.

For Quilting Stained Glass Appliqué

Batting. Select an ultra-thin, non-bearding batting with a ¹⁄₁₆" loft. Thermore® batting was used for all the projects in this book.

Backing fabric. To eliminate the problem of contrasting bobbin thread showing on the top, match the backing to the leading fabric.

Fabric adhesive spray. Using adhesive spray is a convenient method for securing the quilt layers.

Machine needles. For the machine appliqué-quilting stitch, we prefer a #10 jeans/denim needle.

Sewing machine. A well-maintained machine with zigzag capabilities is all you need to complete all the projects. Use an open-toed embroidery foot if you have one.

Thread. Use 2-ply, 60-weight, 100 percent cotton embroidery thread for the top and bobbin in a color that matches the leading fabric.

Fabric Selection

It is important to use a high-thread count, 100 percent cotton fabric for the stained glass leading. The quilts in the projects were made with black Pima cotton. The high thread count produces a cleaner, smoother edge with minimal fraying. Marbled fabrics, batiks, hand-dyes, or textured solids resemble painted glass and are ideal choices for the windowpanes.

Fabric for leading. Black is the most popular choice for the leading, but if you want to create the look of authentic copper or pewter leading, use a batik. It is not necessary to wash the leading fabric. The surface sizing provides added stability to the design. Damp spraying and pressing will remove the sharp center crease.

Fabric requirements. Many of the projects require fabric scraps. If you are purchasing fabric, buy the minimum amount the quilt shop will cut. Purchase extra yardage to selectively cut a particular section of the fabric for specific pattern pieces.

Fused Stained Glass Appliqué

The following instructions for fused stained glass appliqué are standard for all the projects. The Tulip block used in these instructions provides a good introduction to the technique. We recommend starting with this block. Once you have mastered it, you can easily make any of the quilt projects starting on page 19.

Create Stained Glass Leading

You will notice that the pattern is a reverse, or mirror image, of the finished quilt. This is a reverse appliqué technique, which means the fabric pieces are fused to the back of the design. When the appliqué is finished, your quilt will look like the one shown with the project instructions.

Trace Leading Pattern

1. Cut a piece of tracing paper about 2" overall larger than the pattern. Draw a square or rectangular outline the exact dimensions given for the project pattern. Make sure your corners are square (90 degrees). If the pattern has been printed in sections, draw the section lines and number the sections as shown in your project layout diagram. These section lines will help you align your tracing paper with the pattern sections in the book.
2. To hold the paper in place while you trace the pattern, make a few loops of low-tack tape with the sticky side out. Finger press the loops flat to make them like pieces of low-tack double-sided tape.
3. Position the tracing paper on top of the pattern page, aligning the section lines, and secure the tracing paper to the pattern page with your tape loops. Trace the pattern with a mechanical pencil. Be sure to include the piece labels and straight-of-grain lines marked on the pattern.
4. Secure the tracing paper to poster board. Use an extra-fine-point pen to ink the pattern lines. It is not necessary to ink the section lines you drew to help you align your tracing paper with the pattern. You will use this copy as a master pattern to trace

the lines for the leading onto your fusible web and again later to trace the lines onto freezer paper for the stained glass templates.

Trace Pattern on Fusible Web

1. Cut a piece of fusible web about 2" larger overall than your tracing paper. The web has a smooth paper side and a rough fusible side. Position the web with the rough fusible side down over your traced pattern. Tape or staple the web to the poster board to prevent it from shifting as you trace.
2. Use an ultra-fine-point permanent pen to trace the pattern onto the web backing (fig. 1). Start by tracing the pattern outline. Keep the lines as smooth as possible because these are your cutting guides. You'll be happy to know it is much easier to cut a smooth line than it is to trace a smooth line. It is not necessary to write the pattern labels on the web backing.

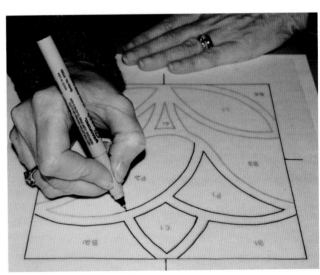

Fig. 1. Trace your pattern onto the fusible web backing.

3. Before removing the finished tracing, double-check that all pattern lines have been traced.
4. Use a ruler and rotary cutter to trim the transfer web ⅜" from the pattern outline. Trim carefully and slowly. The fusible is slippery.

Prepare and Cut Leading Fabric

The care you take in preparing your leading fabric will have everything to do with the success of your stained glass appliqué project.

1. Fold the fabric in half along the straight-of-grain and true up the fabric along the cross grain.

2. With the fabric still folded, cut your binding strips on the cross grain. Then open the fabric and cut your leading piece. If the piece is a rectangle, be sure to cut the length along the straight-of-grain. It's okay to include the selvage in these cuts, because the pieces will be trimmed to size later. Reserve the remaining fabric to use for the backing.

3. Lightly spray the wrong side of your leading fabric with starch, then press it dry.

tip:

Photocopying Versus Tracing

Photocopying a pattern is quicker and easier than tracing. However, be aware there is a likelihood of distortion. Digital photocopiers produce the truest image with minimal distortion. Use a ruler to measure the design in both directions to check the accuracy of the copy.

Photocopy toner is water based and therefore not heat resistant. During the fusing process, the toner may stain light colored fabrics. To avoid this, cover the pattern markings in the open areas with clear cellophane tape.

Another option is to use the scanning software on your computer to reproduce the designs. Inkjet ink can be heat set on paper, which means it will not come off on your fabric during the fusing process.

Fuse Web to Leading Fabric

1. Place your leading fabric right side down on a firm pressing surface, large enough to accommodate the fabric.

2. Carefully align the pattern outline on the transfer web parallel to the fabric edges. Center the web (smooth backing side up) on the wrong side of the leading fabric.

3. Drain your iron of any water and preheat. (See the manufacturer's instructions for your fusible web.).

4. When the transfer web is accurately positioned, secure it with a hot, dry iron. Start at the center and use an up-and-down pressing motion to slow-

ly work toward the outside edges. Do not slide the iron because this will shift the transfer web. Move gradually from one area to the next, slightly overlapping the previously pressed section. Do not miss spots or jump around because this will create air pockets and creases in the transfer web. Hold the iron in position for the slow count of four. Dark fabric shadowing through the transfer web indicates a strong fuse.

5. Press around the edge of the web with the center of the iron to ensure a secure bond along the sides. When the fusing is complete, turn the fabric over and press from the right side. On larger designs, the fabric may appear bubbly. Don't be alarmed; this is normal when a large piece of transfer web is pressed onto fabric. Leave the backing on the fusible web. You will remove it later.

note:

Pressing the transfer web to the fabric is the only part of the technique that is unforgiving. You must be 100 percent accurate in the placement of the transfer web on the fabric before the iron touches it. Once the hot iron rests on it, the web cannot be shifted. It is wise to double-check the web's placement before lifting the iron.

Cut Out Leading

1. Using the pattern as a guide, cut on the pattern lines (fig. 2a). Start in any corner and work toward the center. Do not cut beyond the pattern outline (fig. 2b, page 9).

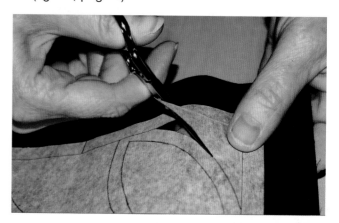

Fig. 2a. Cut out along pattern lines.

Fig. 2b. Start in any corner to cut. Do not cut beyond the pattern outline.

2. To start a cut, make a small fold in the piece to be cut, and make a vertical snip (fig. 3a). Insert the scissors tip and cut toward the traced line (fig. 3b). Do not push the tip of the scissors through at the pen line because this will create a jagged edge.

Fig. 3a. Begin cutting a piece by folding the piece to be cut and snipping into the fold inside the piece.

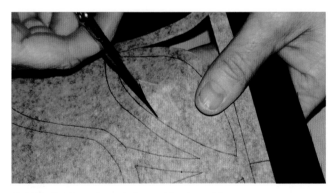

Fig. 3b. Cut from the snip toward the traced line.

3. During the cutting process, the paper backing may lift and separate from the fabric. If it begins to separate on the section you are cutting, stop immediately and re-press. Continuing to cut will produce a jagged edge and narrower leading. As a precaution, give each section a quick press with the Mini Iron™ before starting to cut.

4. If the paper backing separates from leading that has already been cut, do not re-press. Additional pressing will bond the paper to the cut edges. The extra fusing increases the probability of fraying the edge when the paper is removed.

5. Leave the paper backing in place until later when you are ready to fuse the stained glass fabrics. In addition to protecting the raw edge, the paper backing stabilizes the web and makes it easier to handle when auditioning fabric choices.

tip:

Getting Clean Cuts

The quality of the finished product depends on the quality of the cutting. You cannot rely on the finishing stitch to correct or conceal cutting errors. Take your time with the cutting. It is the most important step.

Create Stained Glass Pieces
Combine Pattern Pieces

To cut the stained glass fabrics, you will need templates made from freezer paper. You are going to cover your pattern with the freezer paper and trace the outlines for the stained glass pieces. But before you do this, study the pattern to see if there are adjacent pieces that will be cut from the same fabric. To save some work, you can combine these pieces into one template.

If you are uncertain which pieces to combine or how many pieces to combine, keep this thought in mind: "The safest way is the longest way." You can create problems in the fusing process if too many sections are combined. Remember, the width of the leading line is only ¼". This doesn't leave much margin for error. Large, irregularly shaped pieces are more challenging to trim, position, and fuse. The overall shape of the combined pieces should resemble a square or rectangle. Individual pieces with an odd shape should not be combined with any other sections.

After you have decided which pieces are to be combined, draw lines connecting the leading lines on your original pattern. Then draw a double-ended arrow across the leading lines to indicate that the two pieces have been combined (fig. 4).

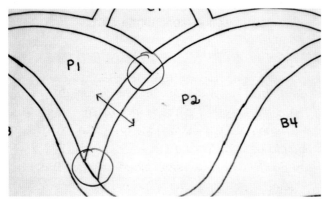

Fig. 4. On your original traced pattern, draw lines through connecting leading. Add a two-way arrow to indicate connected pieces.

Make Freezer-Paper Templates

1. Cut a piece of freezer paper 2" overall larger than your pattern. If the paper curls, place it shiny side down on a large pressing surface and give it a light pressing with a warm, dry iron to flatten it.
2. Place the freezer paper, shiny side down over your pattern and secure it to the poster board. Use a mechanical pencil to trace the individual stained glass templates onto the dull side of freezer paper. Include the label on each piece as well as the grain-line markings.
3. For the combined pieces, it is not necessary to trace the leading lines between the connected pieces (fig. 5).
4. Use a highlighter pen to outline the outside edges. The highlighter is a reminder to use a wider allowance when cutting the outside edge.

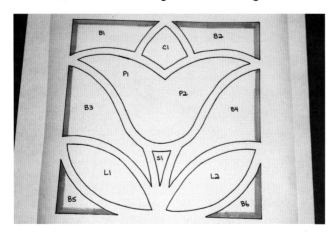

Fig. 5. Trace and label the stained glass pieces on freezer paper and highlight the outside edge.

5. Use craft or paper scissors to cut out the templates along their pencil outlines.

note:

Several patterns contain leading that measures less than ¼". For these, always cut one template and fill the adjacent sections with the same fabric. The leading is not wide enough to support two seam allowances. We will remind you of this in the individual project instructions as it occurs.

Cut Stained Glass Pieces

1. For each stained glass piece, place the template, shiny side down, on the wrong side of the fabric you have selected for that piece.
2. When two or more stained glass pieces are to be cut from the same fabric, position the templates 1" apart. Use a warm, dry iron and press lightly to secure the template to the fabric.
3. Cut the inside stained glass pieces, leaving a ¼" seam allowance around the template. For outside pieces, leave a ½" allowance along the edges marked with highlighter and a ¼" allowance around the unhighlighted edges of the piece (fig. 6).

Fig. 6. Leave a ¼" allowance around inside pieces and a ½" for highlighted outside edges.

note:

A small, 30mm rotary cutter may be used for cuttting the straight lines. Cover the leading line with a clear acrylic ruler. This will protect the web, just in case the cutter slips. Fabric grips or clear, non-slip plastic on the bottom of the ruler will prevent it from slipping on the paper surface. Cut carefully and slowly. The round blade on the rotary cutter makes it difficult to start and stop in a sharp corner. To prevent cutting into the narrow web lines, start and stop the rotary cutter short of the corners, and use scissors to finish the cut.

Fuse Your Stained Glass

Now all your work so far will pay off as you see your stained glass quilt top come together.

Auditioning Fabric Choices

One of the advantages of this technique is the opportunity to audition your fabric choices before they are permanently fused.

1. Place your leading piece right side up on a work surface and slide the pattern pieces underneath. Voila – instant stained glass! (fig. 7)

Fig. 7. Slide stained glass pieces under the leading to audition your fabric choices.

2. If you are unhappy with any of your fabric choices, simply remove the freezer-paper template, select a new fabric, press the template to the new fabric,

and cut a new stained glass piece. The freezer-paper templates can be used over and over again. When you are satisfied with your fabric choices, it's time to fuse the fabric to the web.

note:

Fabric grain is particularly important for large background pieces. Irregularly shaped inside templates that have the grain line marked should be aligned with the straight grain of the fabric. If a large outside piece has not been marked with a grain line, align the straight edge of the template with the fabric's straight grain.

Secure Leading to Traced Pattern

1. Prepare a flat pressing surface large enough to accommodate the whole leading piece. Remove your original traced pattern from the poster board and place it on the pressing surface.

2. Lay your leading piece fusible side up over the pattern. Carefully and slowly remove the paper backing from the fusible web. Be gentle with the raw bias edges, taking care not to stretch them. The white background of the design pattern will accentuate any thread whiskers. Use this opportunity to carefully trim and tidy the leading piece before fusing the fabric pieces (fig. 8). Turn the piece over and repeat this procedure from the right side. Remember, the neater the web, the better the finished product.

Fig. 8. Carefully trim off any whiskers.

3. Position the web on the pattern, matching the ¼" leading lines of both. Use small, low-tack flags to secure the leading piece to the pattern (fig. 9, page 12). It is not necessary to secure the entire piece,

just the lines adjacent to the section being fused. If you have used a flag to secure an underlying leading line on a combined section, remember to remove the flag before fusing the fabric piece.

Fig. 9. Secure the leading to the master pattern with small flags.

Fuse Stained Glass Pieces to Leading

Each fabric piece must be trimmed before it is fused to the web. It is not necessary to trim all sides because the order in which the fabric pieces are fused will determine which seam allowances require trimming.

Each inside web line is shared by two adjacent fabric pieces. If both pieces have a ¼" seam allowance, the first piece fused will take up the entire width of the web line, leaving nothing for the second piece. One seam allowance must be made smaller so both pieces can share the web line.

When the fabric edge is the first one fused to a leading line, it is a primary fuse. It is necessary to trim the fabric edge to half the width of the web line. When the fabric edge is the second one fused, it is not necessary to trim the seam allowance. We will call this the secondary fuse.

Now you're probably asking yourself, "Why didn't I trim all the edges to ⅛" in the first place?" There's a very good explanation for this. An overlapped seam is stronger than two pieces of fabric that butt up against each other. The overlapping seam allowances provide strength and stability to the completed design.

If the fabric edge is a secondary fuse and the seam allowance is larger than ¼", it is still necessary

to trim the seam allowance to ¼" if the adjacent fabric is light and the one being fused is dark. The darker seam allowance will extend past the ¼" leading line and shadow through the lighter fabric.

note:

The seam allowance on outside pattern pieces is larger because the fusible extends ⅜" past the outer edge, and all the fusible should be covered with fabric. The extra width on the fusible and the wider seam allowance creates a stronger, straighter outside edge for finishing with a binding or a border.

1. Start at the bottom corner of the design fusing one piece at a time. Select the appropriate fabric piece by matching the label on the template to the label on the master pattern.
2. Position the fabric piece on the leading. Mark the edges that require trimming with x's, and put check marks on the edges that do not require trimming (fig. 10).

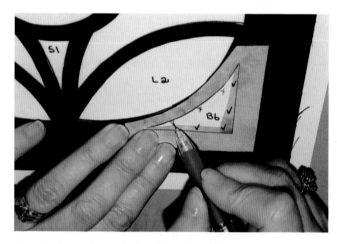

Fig. 10. Use x's to mark the edge to be trimmed and check marks on edges that do not need trimming.

3. Trim the edges marked with x's to a ⅛" allowance. Don't be over zealous with the trimming. You can always re-trim if the seam allowance is too large. Reposition the trimmed piece on the leading to check the seam allowance (fig.11, page 13).
4. Remove the freezer-paper template and use a sewing awl to assist you in fine-tuning the position

of the stained glass piece on the leading. Then fuse the first stained glass piece to the leading.

Fig. 11. Position the trimmed edge over the leading.

5. Repeat steps 1 through 4 for the remaining pieces. Fuse any large or odd-shaped pieces last. By placing all the surrounding pieces first, you will not have to trim the seam allowances on the larger piece. Simply remove the freezer paper, position the fabric, and fuse it in position.

6. When all of the stained glass pieces have been fused into place, give the entire design another firm pressing, front and back, to complete the fusing process.

Cover Exposed Fusible Web

1. Now that the fusing is complete, examine the wrong side of the piece to see if there are any areas of leading that haven't been covered (fig. 13). Where leading fabric shows, there is exposed fusible adhesive. If it isn't covered, the adhesive will melt onto the iron and ironing board cover during the final pressing or when borders are added.

Fig 13. Uncovered areas of leading will have exposed fusible web.

tip:

Pressing Tip

Mini Iron™. The Mini Iron™ is ideal for this technique and after a pair of good quality scissors, it is your next best investment. Set the iron on high and be very careful not to touch the barrel. It is very hot! Place the iron on the edge of the colored fabric where it covers the leading line (fig.12). Allow the iron to sit there for four to five seconds. Use an up-and-down pressing motion to move the iron along the fabric edge. Do not slide the iron as this will shift the fabric piece.

Fig. 12. Use an up-and-down pressing motion to fuse pieces.

Be careful not to touch any of the exposed fusible web with the iron. If you place the Mini Iron™ directly on the fusible it will melt the glue, rendering it useless. Also the melted glue remains on the iron and is transferred to your colored fabrics. The heat from the Mini Iron™ will provide a temporary fuse.

Conventional Iron. If you do not have the Mini Iron™, a conventional iron will do, but you must be very careful. Using only the tip of the iron, press the edge of the fabric piece where it covers the leading line. Do not apply excessive pressure and do not let the iron touch the exposed fusible web. Allow the iron to rest in this position for three seconds. You must allow adequate time for the heat to penetrate the fabric to melt the fusible.

2. To avoid a sticky mess, take a few extra minutes to cover the exposed fusible. If it is a tiny area, don't worry about it. Otherwise, cut a fabric scrap to cover the exposed leading, and fuse the scrap in place (fig. 14).

Fig 14. Cover any uncovered leading with fabric scraps to cover exposed fusible web.

Touch Up Fused Pieces

1. Take a few minutes to inspect the back of the quilt top. Hold the quilt top up to a light. Look for any weak areas where the fabric is secured by only a few threads. If this weak area is not strengthened, the fabric may fray and separate from the web during the finishing process. To reinforce these areas, cut a ¼" x 1" strip of fusible woven interfacing (not to be confused with fusible transfer web). On the back of the quilt, position the interfacing, fusible side down, over the area. The interfacing acts as an extension for the short piece. It overlaps the edge of the narrow seam allowance joining it to the fabric on the opposite side.

2. Check for edges that are not securely fused. Gently lift the raw edges of all the stained glass pieces. If the fabric peels back easily, you can try re-pressing with a hot iron. Allow the fabric and fusible to cool before testing again. If the edge is still loose, it can be secured with fabric glue. We use Rox-anne's Glue Baste-It™. Press the loose fabric to the underlying fabric. Allow the glue to dry, and then retest.

3. Trim your stained glass quilt top to the finished dimensions given in your project instructions.

Finishing Your Quilting

Use your favorite techniques for adding borders and assembling the quilt layers. Here are some of our favorite ways of finishing a quilt.

All of the projects presented can be made larger by adding borders. A pieced border or a border with mitered corners is the perfect finishing touch for stained glass quilts. One word of caution: Don't allow the border treatment to overpower the design. We intentionally kept the borders simple because we did not want to detract from the beauty of the stained glass.

Baste the Quilt Layers

Fabric adhesive spray for quilt basting is an excellent alternative to 1" safety pins. Read the label for manufacturer's instructions specific to their product. Follow these simple rules for successful use of the adhesive spray. Work on one half of the quilt at a time and always spray the batting, not the fabric. Be safety conscious. Spray in a well ventilated area and cover your nose and mouth while spraying.

1. Cut the batting the same size as the backing. Place the backing fabric wrong side up on a flat work surface and secure the four sides with masking tape. Secure the length of grain first and then the cross grain. The backing should be taut but not stretched. Pulling too tightly will distort the fabric and cause puckering when the tape is removed.

2. Place the batting over the backing. Working from the center out, smooth out the extra fullness and any wrinkles. Protect the work surface by placing disposable papers around the batting edge.

3. Fold the batting in half. Hold the can 12" away from the batting and spray in 12" intervals. Unfold the batting and reposition the sprayed half on the backing and hand press it in place to secure the batting to the backing. Repeat this procedure for the other half of the batting.

4. Center the quilt top on the batting. Smooth the quilt top, being careful not to stretch or distort it. Cover the exposed batting with disposable paper to keep adhesive spray off it. Fold the quilt top in half.

5. Spray the batting that will be under the quilt top. Unfold the quilt top onto the sprayed batting, then hand press to secure the quilt top to the batting. Repeat this process to secure the second half of the quilt top.

tip:

Brenda's Tip to Avoid a Sticky Mess

It is important to use disposable papers to cover the exposed batting when you spray-baste the quilt top. I didn't do this the first time I used the product and sprayed the topside of the batting from edge to edge. The excess batting at the quilt edge stuck to itself; it stuck to the quilt; it stuck to the sewing machine; and it stuck to me!

Quilting and Appliqué Stitching All-in-One

Secure the quilt layers. Several of the projects have large irregular-shaped sections. To prevent ripples in the top layer, we recommend quilting all of these sections with a walking foot and straight stitch before doing the appliqué stitch. Start at the center of your quilt top and stitch as close to the raw edge of the leading fabric as you can without stitching into it.

Choose your stitch. The machine appliqué and quilting are done at the same time. What a time-saver! You can use a zigzag foot, but an open-toe embroidery foot provides better visibility. The raw edges of the leading fabric can be finished with a blanket or zigzag stitch. Our preference is the blanket stitch that shifts to the left for the zigzag portion of the stitch.

Some machines have two choices of blanket stitch – a single stitched or double stitched. Select the single-stitch option, then set the width to 1.5 and the length to 1.8 approximately. For the zigzag stitch set the width to 1.5 and the length to 1.5.

Before stitching on your quilt do a practice piece to perfect the securing stitch and stitch size. Cut several ¼" strips of black fabric from the leftover cuttings and fuse the strips in the shape of a square or triangle onto scrap fabric. Create a quilt sandwich with the same batting and backing used in your quilt. Read through the steps below, then make your practice piece. When you have perfected the stitch width and length, record the machine settings for future use. If your machine has stitch memory, preset the settings for the appliqué stitch and the straight stitch. Start with the straight stitch and then select the appliqué stitch. The needle position should be identical for both stitches.

1. The purpose of the appliqué stitch is functional, not decorative. It is used to finish the raw edges of the leading fabrics and to hold the three layers together. Ideally, the stitching should blend into the leading and become virtually invisible. Start sewing in the center of the quilt, in the corner of a colored fabric.

2. Insert the needle into the colored fabric alongside the inside right edge of the black fabric. The left

side of the needle should graze the raw edge of the black fabric but not pierce it. Sewing into the raw edge of the leading will shred it. Bring the bobbin thread to the top side and hold onto both threads as you take the first stitch. This avoids a snarl on the back and prevents sewing over the bobbin thread. Begin sewing with a very small straight stitch. Sew three or four stitches, backstitch the same amount, then select the appliqué stitch.

Quilt the Border

Many of the designs in this book have a wider black border. If you choose to quilt the border, you can create a simple yet very effective quilting design by continuing the flow of the leading lines into the border.

1. Cut strips of white freezer paper the same width as the border. Use your Mini-Iron to heat press the freezer paper to the border.

tip:

Make Perfect Appliqué Stitches

For straight, even stitches keep the presser foot parallel to the edge of the leading fabric (Fig. 15). Sew at a reduced speed to ensure the accurate placement of each stitch. On curves, it is necessary to pivot often to keep the foot parallel to the edge of the leading fabric. To do this, stop stitching with the needle down on the right side of the stitch, lift the presser foot, and rotate the fabric.

Fig. 15. Keep the presser foot parallel to the edge of the leading fabric.

On straight edges, sew all the way into the corner before turning the quilt. It may be necessary to reduce the stitch length to accomplish this. A more convenient way is to gently pull back on the quilt top with your fingertips as you approach the corner. The added resistance prevents the fabric from advancing and automatically creates a smaller stitch.

If you misjudge the curve or the machine goes off course, there will be a noticeable space between the stitch line and the fabric edge. Black thread on a light background accentuates stitches that are out of alignment whereas dark fabric is a little more forgiving. If the space between the stitches and the fabric edge is considerable, stop sewing and remove the stitches. Insert the needle at the last stitch and continue sewing. Do not use securing stitches in the middle of a leading line. When the section is complete draw the loose threads to the back of the quilt, knot, and bury the ends.

End your stitching in the same corner you started. Backstitch four or five small straight stitches to secure the seam. Snip the top threads close to the quilt top. At this point, you can move to another section before cutting the bobbin thread. This can be done later after multiple sections are stitched. Stitch each stained glass pane individually; in other words, don't stitch across the leading to begin a new pane.

2. Locate a leading line that ends at the border edge. Visualize the flow of the leading if it extended to the outer edge of the border. Would it be straight or would it curve? Use a pencil to draw an extension of the leading line onto the freezer paper. Make the width of the extension the same width as the leading.

3. Cut out the extension, and press the freezer paper onto the border. Use a walking foot and a straight stitch to quilt along the edge of the freezer paper. Start at the inside edge, do a U-turn in the batting, and sew down the opposite side towards the inside edge (fig. 16).

Fig. 16. Use freezer-paper extensions to mark quilting lines.

4. It is not necessary to extend all the web lines. Start with the main ones and add more to balance the density of the quilting.

tip:

Use a New Needle

For quilting your stained-glass-appliqué quilt, always start with a new #10 jeans/denim needle. Stitching through the quilt layers as well as the fused web can be hard on your needle. To maintain stitch quality, put in a new needle halfway through the project.

Square Up Your Quilt

To ensure that your quilt hangs square, run a hand-basting stitch catching all three layers. The basting stitches will be within the binding seam allowance and will not have to be removed after the binding is attached. Baste each side separately.

1. Cut a single strand of hand-quilting thread 15" longer than one side of the quilt. With stitches ¼" long, baste ⅛" from the quilt edge. Baste to the end of the side but do not tie off or anchor the thread. Remove the needle and baste the remaining three sides in the same way.

2. Lay the quilt on a flat surface and gently pull on the threads to snug up the edges slightly so the sides of the quilt are the same length and the top and bottom are the same length. Lay a square ruler in the corner to check that the corners are 90 degrees.

3. Once your quilt is square, secure your basting threads by wrapping the loose ends in a figure 8 around a straight pin placed in the batting ½" beyond the quilt edge.

tip:

Using Your Machine's Stitch Memory

If your machine has stitch memory, preset the settings for the appliqué stitch and the straight stitch. Start with the straight stitch and then select the appliqué stitch. The needle position should be identical for both stitches.

1. Cut enough 1" fabric strips to go around the quilt. Press the strips in half lengthwise, wrong sides together.
2. Measure the length of the quilt and cut two strips to this measurement. Align the raw edges of a folded strip with each quilt side and pin the strip in place. With a walking foot and a scant ¼" seam allowance, sew the tuck to the quilt edge. A narrower seam allowance will ensure that no part of the stitch line will be visible after the binding is added.
3. Repeat this procedure for the top and bottom edges. The tuck goes from edge to edge, overlapping the side tucks.

Bind Edges and Sign Off

Add binding to your quilt using your favorite method. Then be sure to sign off on your quilt by attaching a label. This is the same as putting your signature on the quilt. In addition to your name, include the date, where you live, the name of the quilt, who the quilt was made for, and possibly the reason for making the quilt such as a special birthday or anniversary. Just think, 100 years from now, if someone comes across your quilt in a box of treasures, they'll know who made the quilt and why.

tip:

Design Option: Adding a Fabric Tuck

A tuck of brightly colored fabric between the quilt and the binding is a clever design option that creates the illusion of a narrow accent border with minimal work (fig. 17). The fabric tuck goes on after the quilt edge is basted and before the binding is added.

Fig. 17. A fabric tuck next to the binding accents the quilt's outer edge.

Tulip Garden

Pattern Size 7" x 7" • Quilt Size 26½" x 26½"
Pattern on page 21.

Materials for Four-Block Quilt

high-thread-count black for leading . . . . ½ yd.
tulip, pattern P (each block) . . . . ⅛ yd.
tulip centers, pattern C . . . . ⅛ yd.
leaves, pattern L . . . . ⅛ yd.
sky, pattern B . . . . ¼ yd.
cornerstones . . . . ⅛ yd.
sashing . . . . ¼ yd.
border and binding . . . . ⅝ yd.
backing . . . . ⅞ yd.
ultra-thin batting . . . . ⅞ yd.
fusible transfer web . . . . ½ yd.
poster board, tracing paper, and freezer paper

Create Stained Glass Leading pages 7–9

Page numbers refer to the detailed instructions on Fused Stained Glass Appliqué.

These are the instructions for making a single stained glass Tulip block. You can make four Tulip blocks and join them with sashing and a border to make the TULIP GARDEN quilt pictured on page 19.

1. The pattern outline for TULIP GARDEN is 7" x 7". Cut a piece of tracing paper about 2" overall larger than your pattern outline. Trace the pattern on page 21 on the tracing paper and secure the tracing to poster board to make a master pattern.
2. Cut a piece of fusible web about 4" overall larger than your pattern outline. Trace the master pattern onto the fusible web backing. Trim the web, leaving ⅜" extra around all four sides of the pattern outline.
3. Prepare your leading fabric and cut a 10" x 10" square on the straight of grain for the leading.
4. Fuse the web tracing in the center of the leading fabric. Then cut out the leading lines.

Create Stained Glass Pieces pages 9–11

1. Before cutting the freezer-paper templates for the stained glass, check to see if any pattern pieces can be combined to reduce the number of templates you will need to cut.
2. Cut a piece of freezer paper 2" overall larger than your master pattern. Finish making your freezer-paper templates.
3. Cut out your stained glass pieces, leaving the appropriate seam allowances.
4. Audition your stained glass fabric choices. Then secure the leading to the traced pattern.

Fuse Your Stained Glass pages 11–14

1. To finish your stained glass quilt, start at a bottom corner of the design and position and fuse each piece in place to the back of the leading.
2. Give your stained glass design a final check by covering any exposed fusible web and touching up your fused pieces.
3. To trim your tulip block to size, trim about ½" off each side of your leading fabric to make a square 9" x 9".

Add Sashing and a Border

1. If you are making a quilt with four Tulip blocks, cut twelve 2" x 9" sashing strips and nine 2" x 2"

cornerstones.

2. Refer to the quilt photo. Make a block row by sewing two blocks and three sashing strips together. Make two block rows.

3. Make a sashing row by joining three cornerstones to two sashing strips. Make three sashing rows.

4. Join your block rows and sashing rows. Then add border strips, cut 3" wide.

Finish Your Stained Glass Quilt pages 14–18

To prepare your quilt top for finishing, see the tips and instructions for basting the quilt layers. Secure your fused stained glass pieces by quilting and appliqué stitching all in one, then see the tips for quilting the border. Add the finishing touches by squaring up your quilt, binding, and signing it.

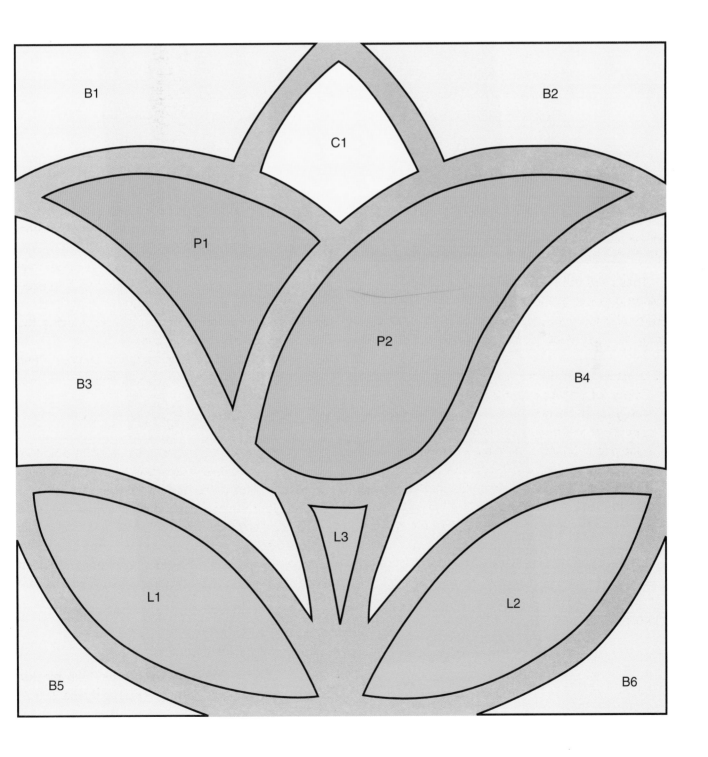

Golden Daffodil

Pattern Size 8¼" x 18⅛" • Quilt Size 11¾" x 21⅝"
Pattern on pages 24–26.

Materials

high-thread-count black for leading, backing, and binding	1 yd.
flower, pattern D	⅛ yd.
leaves, pattern L	⅛ yd. each of two different greens
background, pattern S	¼ yd.
right and bottom border, pattern B	⅛ yd.
border tuck	⅛ yd.
ultra-thin batting	½ yd.
fusible transfer web	⅓ yd.
poster board, tracing paper, and freezer paper	

Create Stained Glass Leading pages 7–9

Page numbers refer to the detailed instructions on Fused Stained Glass Appliqué.

1. The pattern outline for GOLDEN DAFFODIL is 8¼" x 18 ⅛". Cut a piece of tracing paper about 2" overall larger than your pattern outline. Trace the pattern on pages 24–26 on the tracing paper and secure the tracing to poster board to make a master pattern.
2. Cut a piece of fusible web about 4" overall larger than your pattern outline. Trace the master pattern onto the fusible web backing. Trim the web, leaving ⅜" extra around all four sides of the pattern outline.
3. Cut two 2¼" binding strips from the leading fabric, then unfold the fabric and cut a rectangle on the straight of grain 13" x 22⅞" for the leading lines. Save the remaining fabric for your backing.
4. Fuse the web tracing to the leading fabric. Then cut out the leading lines.

Create Stained Glass Pieces pages 9–11

1. Before cutting the freezer-paper templates for the stained glass, check to see if any pattern pieces can be combined to reduce the number of templates you will need to cut.
2. Cut a piece of freezer paper 2" overall larger than your master pattern. Finish making your freezer-

paper templates.
3. Cut out your stained glass pieces, leaving the appropriate seam allowances.
4. Audition your stained glass fabric choices. Then secure the leading to the traced pattern.

Fuse Your Stained Glass pages 11–14

1. To finish your stained glass quilt, start at a bottom corner of the design and position and fuse each piece in place to the back of the leading.
2. Give your stained glass a final check by covering any exposed fusible web and touching up your fused pieces.
3. Trim your quilt top to 11¾" x 21⅝", leaving a 1¾" border around all sides of the pattern outline. You will be trimming approximately ⅝" off each side of your leading fabric.

Finish Your Stained Glass Quilt pages 14–18

To prepare your quilt top for finishing, see the tips and instructions for basting the quilt layers. Secure your fused stained glass pieces by quilting and appliqué stitching all in one, then see the tips for quilting the border. Add the finishing touches by squaring up your quilt, adding a fabric tuck, binding, and signing it.

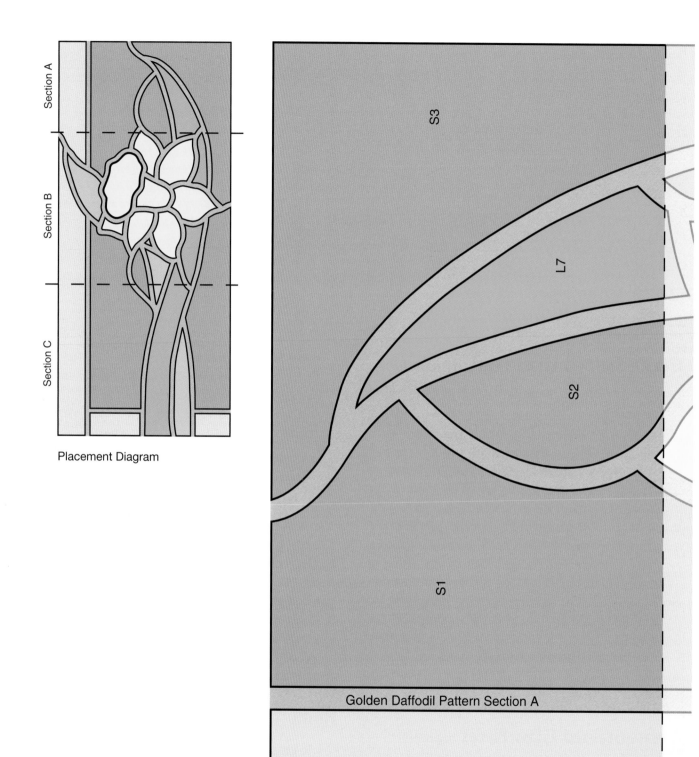

Section A

Section B

Section C

Placement Diagram

S3

L7

S2

S1

Golden Daffodil Pattern Section A

B1

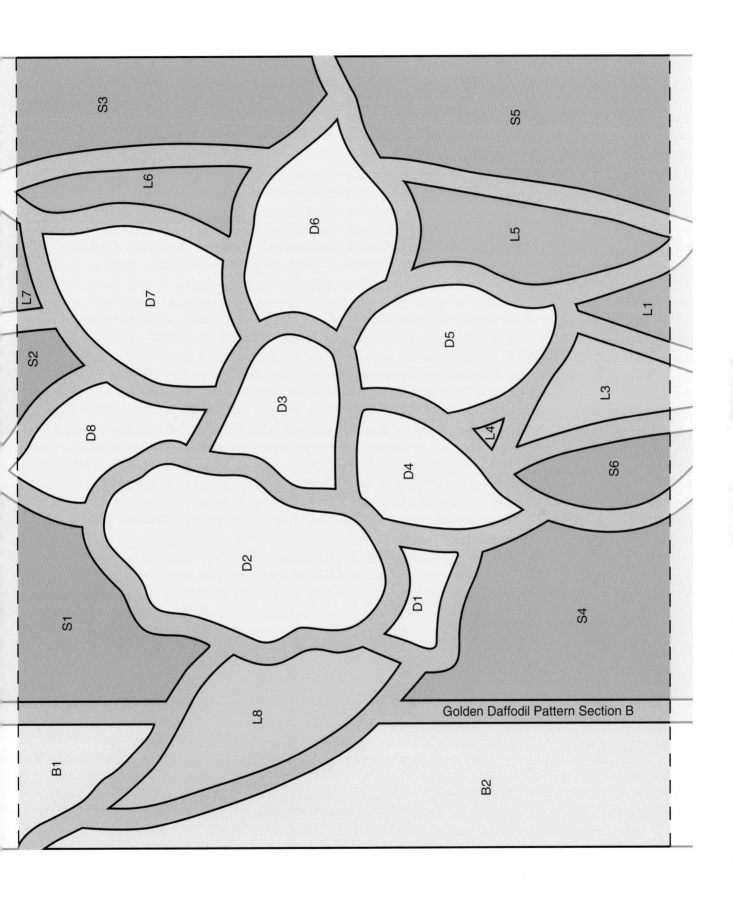

Golden Daffodil Pattern Section B

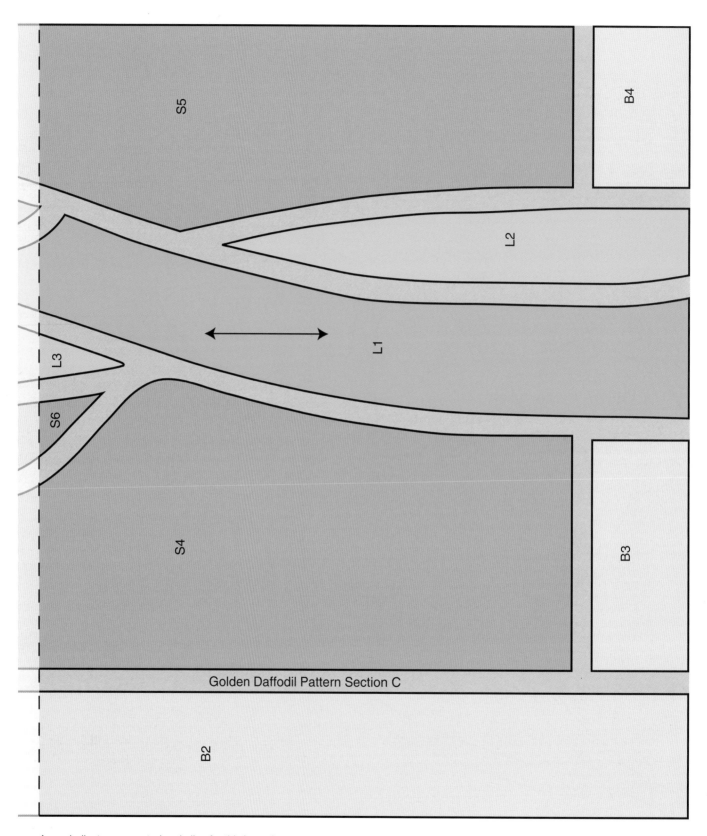

Golden Daffodil Pattern Section C

Arrow indicates suggested grain line for this long piece.

Yukon, My Sanctuary

Pattern Size 14¾" x 19" • Quilt Size 17¼" x 21½"
Pattern on pages 29–32.

Materials

high-thread-count black for leading, backing, and binding	1 yd.
large hills, pattern D	¼ yd. each of three different greens
small hills and trees, patterns G and T	⅛ yd. of three different greens
water, pattern W	¼ yd.
sky, pattern S	¼ yd.
clouds, pattern C	⅛ yd.
border tuck	⅛ yd.
ultra-thin batting	½ yd.
fusible transfer web	⅝ yd.
poster board, tracing paper, and freezer paper	

Create Stained Glass Leading pages 7–9

Page numbers refer to the detailed instructions on Fused Stained Glass Appliqué.

1. The pattern outline for YUKON, MY SANCTUARY is 14¾" x 19". Cut a piece of tracing paper about 2" overall larger than your pattern outline. Trace the pattern on pages 29–32 on the tracing paper and secure the tracing to poster board to make a master pattern.

2. Cut a piece of fusible web about 4" overall larger than your pattern outline. Trace the master pattern onto the fusible web backing. Trim the web, leaving ⅜" extra around all four sides of the pattern outline.

3. Cut two 2¼" binding strips from the leading fabric, then unfold the fabric and cut a rectangle on the straight of grain 18¼" x 22½" for the leading lines. Save the remaining fabric for your backing.

4. Fuse the web tracing to the leading fabric. Then cut out the leading.

Create Stained Glass Pieces pages 9–11

1. Before cutting the freezer-paper templates for the stained glass, check to see if any pattern pieces can be combined to reduce the number of templates you will need to cut.

2 Cut a piece of freezer paper 2" overall larger than your master pattern. Finish making your freezer-paper templates.

3. Cut out your stained glass pieces, leaving the appropriate seam allowances.

4. Audition your stained glass fabric choices. Then secure the leading to the traced pattern.

Fuse Your Stained Glass pages 11–14

1. To finish your stained glass quilt, start at a bottom corner of the design and position and fuse each piece in place to the back of the leading.

2. Give your stained glass a final check by covering any exposed fusible web and touching up your fused pieces.

3. Trim your quilt top to 17¼" x 21½", leaving a 1¼" border around all sides of the pattern outline. You will be trimming approximately ½" off each side of your leading fabric.

Finish Your Stained Glass Quilt pages 14–18

To prepare your quilt top for finishing, see the tips and instructions for basting the quilt layers. Secure your fused stained glass pieces by quilting and appliqué stitching all in one, then see the tips for quilting the border. Add the finishing touches by squaring up your quilt, adding a fabric tuck, binding, and signing it.

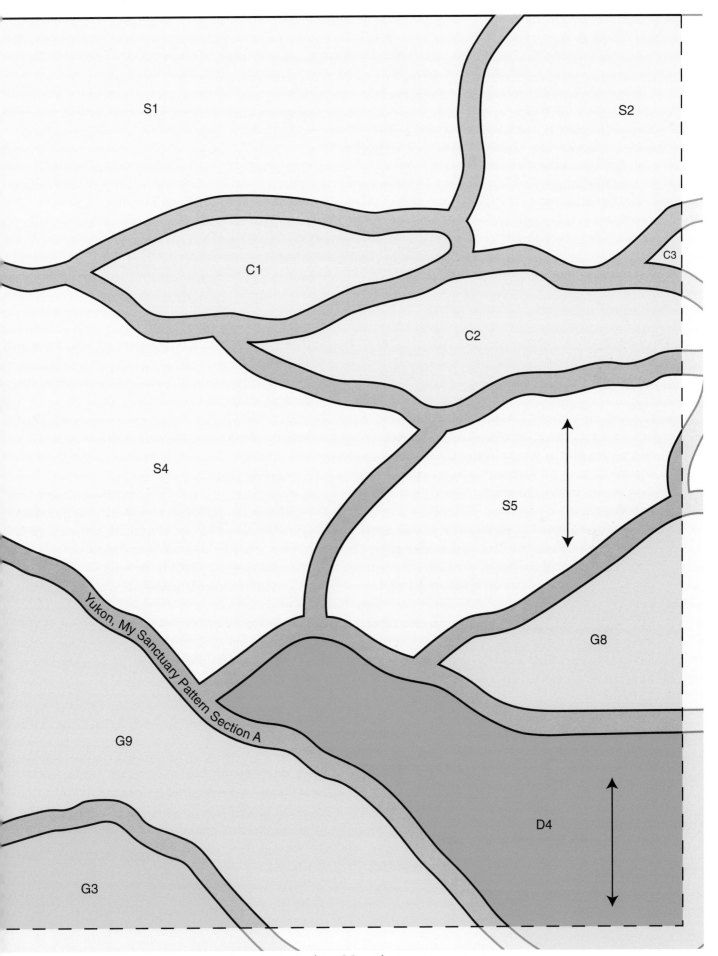

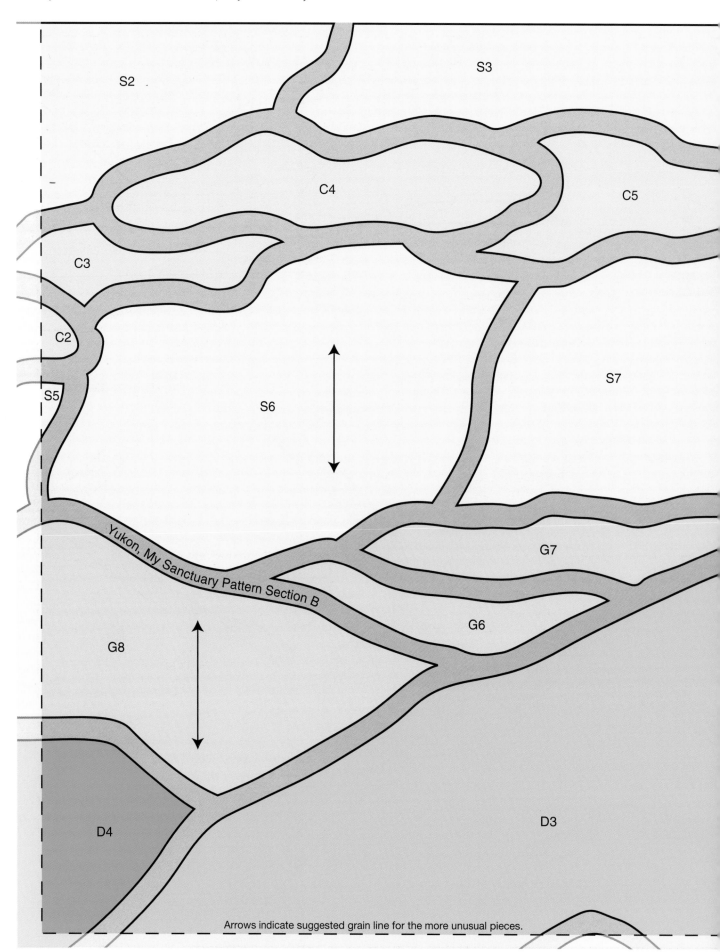

S2

S3

C4

C5

C3

C2

S5

S6

S7

Yukon, My Sanctuary Pattern Section B

G7

G6

G8

D4

D3

Arrows indicate suggested grain line for the more unusual pieces.

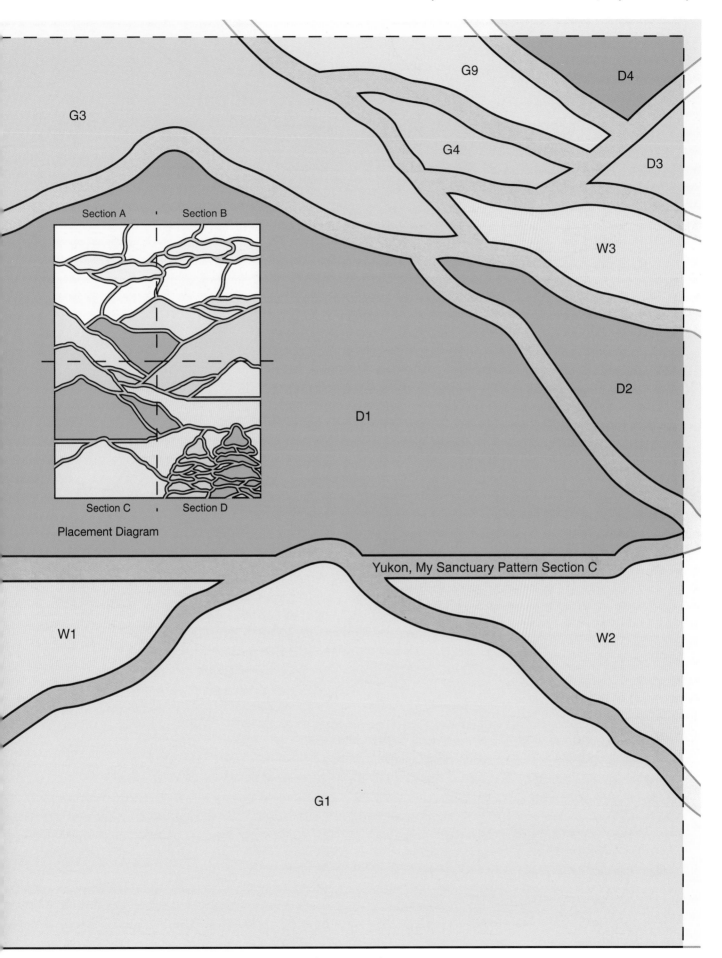

G9

D4

G3

G4

D3

Section A Section B

W3

Section C Section D

D2

D1

Placement Diagram

Yukon, My Sanctuary Pattern Section C

W1

W2

G1

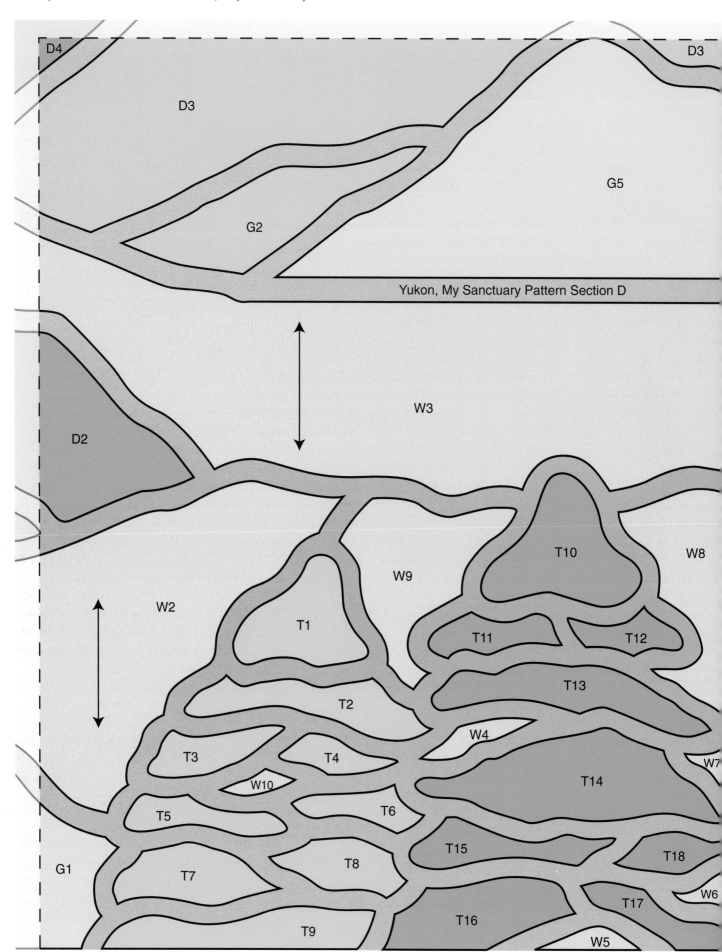

Yukon, My Sanctuary Pattern Section D

Morning Call

Pattern Size 15" x 18¾" • Quilt Size 18" x 21¾"
Pattern on pages 35–38.

Materials

high-thread-count black for leading, backing, and binding . . . . .1 yd.
tail and wing, pattern T . . . . .¼ yd.
breast and body, pattern C . . . . .⅛ yd.
comb, wattles, legs and feet, pattern F . . . . .⅛ yd.
eye, pattern E . . . . .small scrap
beak, pattern A . . . . .small scrap
steps, pattern S . . . . .⅛ yd.
corner squares, pattern D . . . . .small scrap
background, pattern B . . . . .¼ yd.
border tuck . . . . .⅛ yd.
fusible transfer web . . . . .⅝ yd.
ultra-thin batting . . . . .½ yd.
poster board, tracing paper, and freezer paper

Create Stained Glass Leading pages 7–9

Page numbers refer to the detailed instructions on Fused Stained Glass Appliqué.

1. The pattern outline for MORNING CALL is 15" x 18¾". Cut a piece of tracing paper about 2" overall larger than your pattern outline. Trace the pattern on pages 35–38 on the tracing paper and secure the tracing to poster board to make a master pattern.
2. Cut a piece of fusible web about 4" overall larger than your pattern outline. Trace the master pattern onto the fusible web backing. Trim the web, leaving ⅜" extra around all four sides of the pattern outline.
3. Cut two 2¼" binding strips from the leading fabric, then unfold the fabric and cut a rectangle on the straight of grain 19" x 22¾" for the leading lines. Save the remaining fabric for your backing.
4. Fuse the web tracing to the leading fabric. Then cut out the leading lines.

Create Stained Glass Pieces pages 9–11

1. The web line in the rooster's eye is less than ¼" wide. To get a good fuse, trace the eye as one template and cut the eye as one piece. Before making the other freezer-paper templates for the stained glass, check to see if any pattern pieces can be combined to reduce the number of templates you will need to cut.

2. Cut a piece of freezer paper about 2" larger overall than your master pattern. Finish making your freezer-paper templates.
3. Cut out your stained glass pieces, leaving the appropriate seam allowances.
4. Audition your stained glass fabric choices. Then secure the leading to the traced pattern.

Fuse Your Stained Glass pages 11–14

1. To finish your stained glass quilt, start at a bottom corner of the design and position and fuse each piece in place to the back of the leading.
2. Give your stained glass a final check by covering any exposed fusible web and touching up your fused pieces.
3. Trim your quilt top to 18" x 21¾", leaving a 1½" border around all sides of the pattern outline. You will be trimming approximately ½" off each side of your leading fabric.

Finish Your Stained Glass Quilt pages 14–18

To prepare your quilt top for finishing, see the tips and instructions for basting the quilt layers. Secure your fused stained glass pieces by quilting and appliqué stitching all in one, then see the tips for quilting the border. Add the finishing touches by squaring up your quilt, adding a fabric tuck, binding, and signing it.

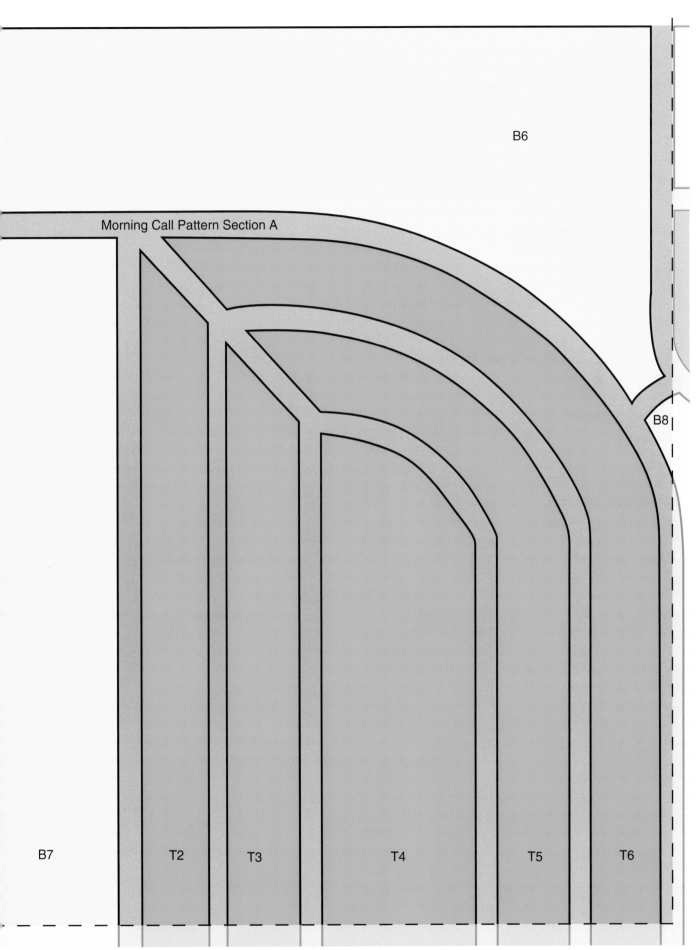

B6

Morning Call Pattern Section A

B8

B7

T2

T3

T4

T5

T6

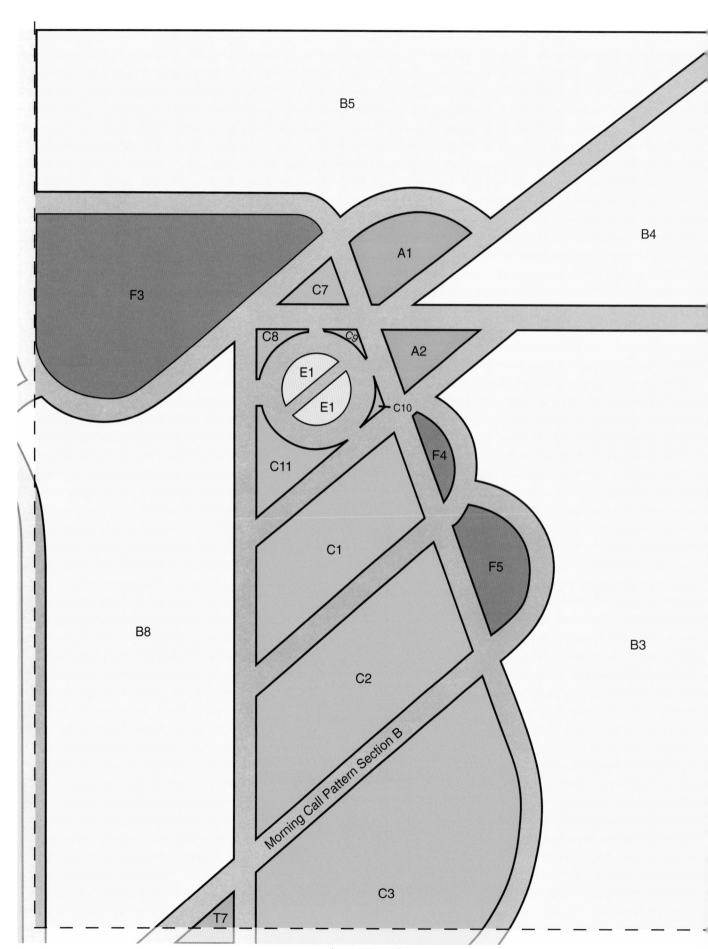

B5

B4

F3

A1

C7

C8   C9

A2

E1

E1

C10

C11

F4

C1

F5

B8

C2

B3

Morning Call Pattern Section B

C3

T7

B7

T2

T3

T4

T5

T6

Morning Call Pattern Section C

C4

C5

C6

T1

B1

F1

D1

S1

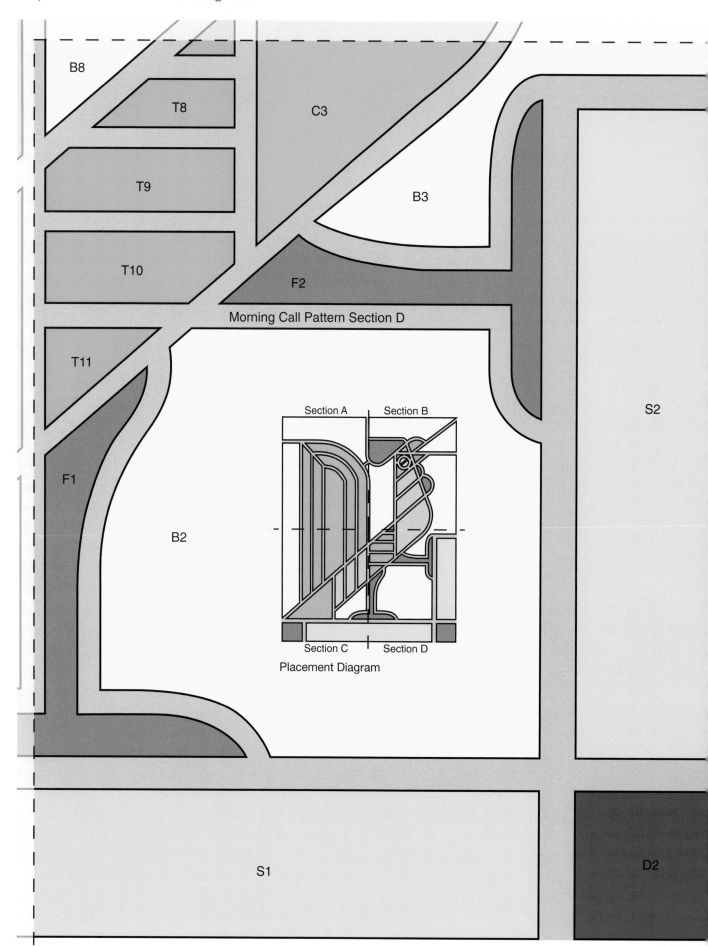

B8

T8

C3

T9

B3

T10

F2

Morning Call Pattern Section D

T11

Section A   Section B

S2

F1

B2

Placement Diagram

Section C   Section D

S1

D2

It's a Cat's Life

Pattern Size 15" x 15" • Quilt Size 18" x 18"
Pattern on pages 41–44.

Materials

high-thread-count black fabric for leading, backing, and binding . . . . ⅞ yd.
Log Cabin center and cat's tail, pattern C . . . . ⅛ yd.
gold/red logs, pattern R . . . . ⅛ yd. each of four shades
green logs, pattern G . . . . ⅛ yd. each of four shades
fall leaves, pattern F . . . . ⅛ yd.
summer leaves, pattern S . . . . ⅛ yd.
fusible transfer web . . . . ½ yd.
ultra-thin batting . . . . ⅝ yd.
poster board, tracing paper, and freezer paper

Create Stained Glass Leading pages 7–9

Page numbers refer to the detailed instructions on Fused Stained Glass Appliqué.

1. The pattern outline for IT'S A CAT'S LIFE is 15" x 15". Cut a piece of tracing paper about 2" overall larger than your pattern outline. Trace the pattern on pages 41–44 on the tracing paper and secure the tracing to poster board to make a master pattern.

2. Cut a piece of fusible web about 4" overall larger than your pattern outline. Trace the master pattern onto the fusible web backing. Trim the web, leaving ⅜" extra around all four sides of the pattern outline.

3. Cut two 2¼" binding strips from the leading fabric, then unfold the fabric and cut a square 19" x 19" for the leading. Save the remaining fabric for your backing.

4. Fuse the web tracing to the leading fabric. Then cut out the leading lines.

Create Stained Glass Pieces pages 9–11

1. The web line in the cat's body is less than ¼" wide. To get a good fuse, trace the cat's body as one template and cut it as one piece. Before cutting the freezer-paper templates for the stained glass, check to see if any pattern pieces can be combined to reduce the number of templates you will need to cut.

2. Cut a piece of freezer paper about 2" larger overall than your master pattern. Finish making your freezer-paper templates.

3. Cut out your stained glass pieces, leaving the appropriate seam allowances.

4. Audition your stained glass fabric choices. Then secure the leading to the traced pattern.

Fuse Your Stained Glass pages 11–14

1. To finish your stained glass quilt, start at a bottom corner of the design and position and fuse each piece in place to the back of the leading.

2. Give your stained glass a final check by covering any exposed fusible web and touching up your fused pieces.

3. Trim your quilt top to 18" x 18", leaving a 1½" border around all sides of the pattern outline. You will be trimming approximately ½" off each side of your leading fabric.

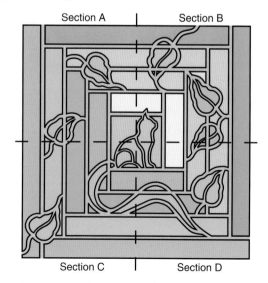

Section A   Section B

Section C   Section D

Placement Diagram

Finish Your Stained Glass Quilt pages 14–18

To prepare your quilt top for finishing, see the tips and instructions for basting the quilt layers. Secure your fused stained glass pieces by quilting and appliqué stitching all in one, then see the tips for quilting the border. Add the finishing touches by squaring up your quilt, binding, and signing it.

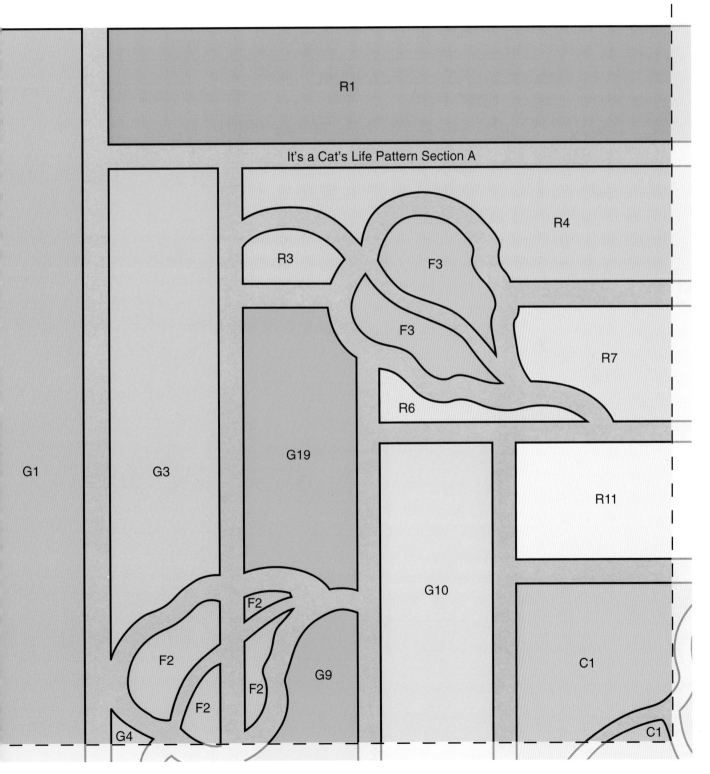

It's a Cat's Life Pattern Section A

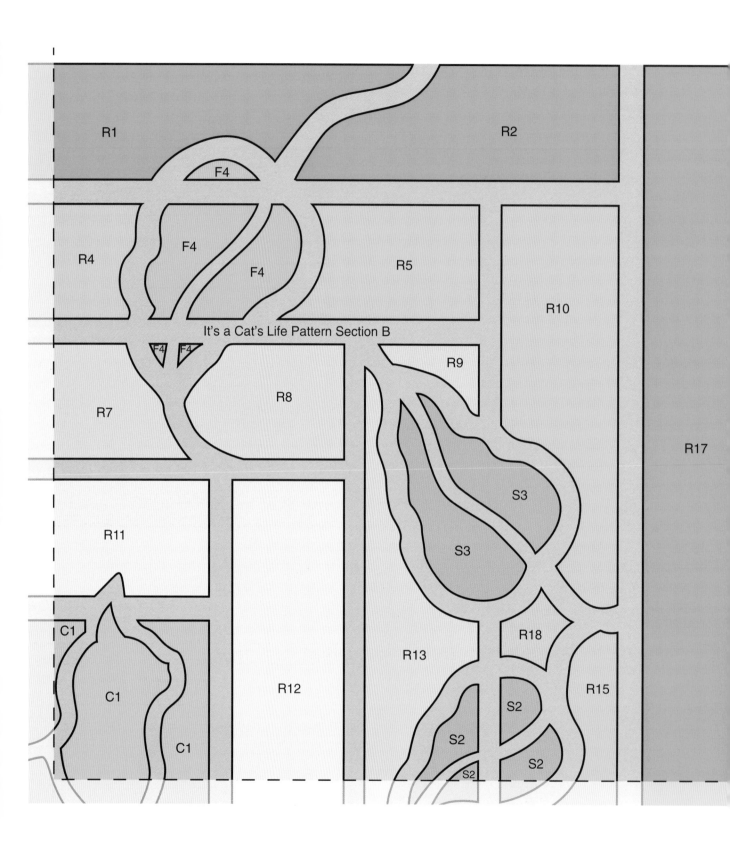

It's a Cat's Life Pattern Section B

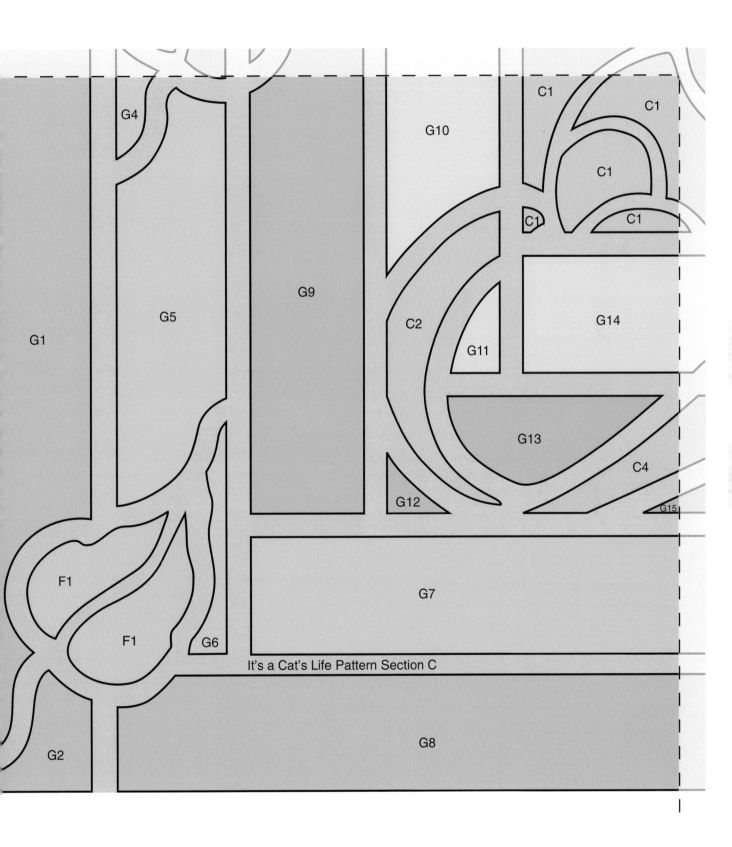

It's a Cat's Life Pattern Section C

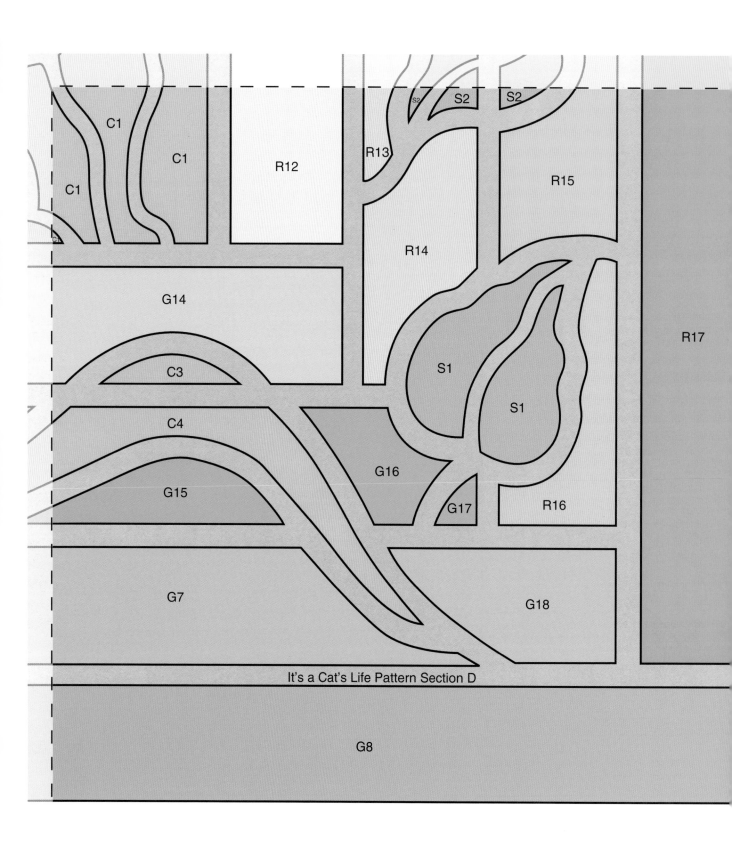

It's a Cat's Life Pattern Section D

Northern Wonders

Pattern Size 15" x 19" • Quilt Size 15½" x 19½"
Pattern on pages 47–50.

Materials

high-thread-count black fabric for leading, backing, and binding	⅞ yd.
night sky, pattern S	⅛ yd.
water, pattern W	⅛ yd.
green hills and corner design, pattern L	¼ yd. total of 3 or more different greens
moon, pattern M	a scrap
clouds, pattern C	⅛ yd.
Northern Lights, pattern N	⅛ yd.
ultra-thin batting	½ yd.
fusible transfer web	½ yd.

Create Stained Glass Leading pages 7–9

Page numbers refer to the detailed instructions on Fused Stained Glass Appliqué.

1. The pattern outline for NORTHERN WONDERS is 15" x 19". Cut a piece of tracing paper about 2" overall larger than your pattern outline. Trace the pattern on pages 47-50 on the tracing paper and secure the tracing to poster board to make a master pattern.
2. Cut a piece of fusible web about 4" overall larger than your pattern outline. Trace the master pattern onto the fusible web backing. Trim the web, leaving ⅜" extra around all four sides of the pattern outline.
3. Cut two 2¼" binding strips from the leading fabric, then unfold the fabric and cut a rectangle on the straight of grain 17" x 21" for the leading lines. Save the remaining fabric for your backing.
4. Fuse the web tracing to the leading fabric. Then cut out the leading lines.

Create Stained Glass Pieces pages 9–11

1. Before making the freezer-paper templates for the stained glass, check to see if any pattern pieces can be combined to reduce the number of templates you will need to cut.
2. Cut a piece of freezer paper about 2" larger overall than your master pattern. Finish making your freezer-paper templates.
3. Cut out your stained glass pieces, leaving the appropriate seam allowances.
4. Audition your stained glass fabric choices. Then secure the leading to the traced pattern.

Fuse Your Stained Glass pages 11–14

1. To finish your stained glass quilt, start at a bottom corner of the design and position and fuse each piece in place to the back of the leading.
2. Give your stained glass a final check by covering any exposed fusible web and touching up your fused pieces.
3. Trim your quilt top to 15½" x 19½", leaving a ¼" border around all sides of the pattern outline. You will be trimming approximately ¾" off each side of your leading fabric.

Finish Your Stained Glass Quilt pages 14–18

To prepare your quilt top for finishing, see the tips and instructions for basting the quilt layers. Secure your fused stained glass pieces by quilting and appliqué stitching all in one, then see the tips for quilting the border. Add the finishing touches by squaring up your quilt, binding, and signing it.

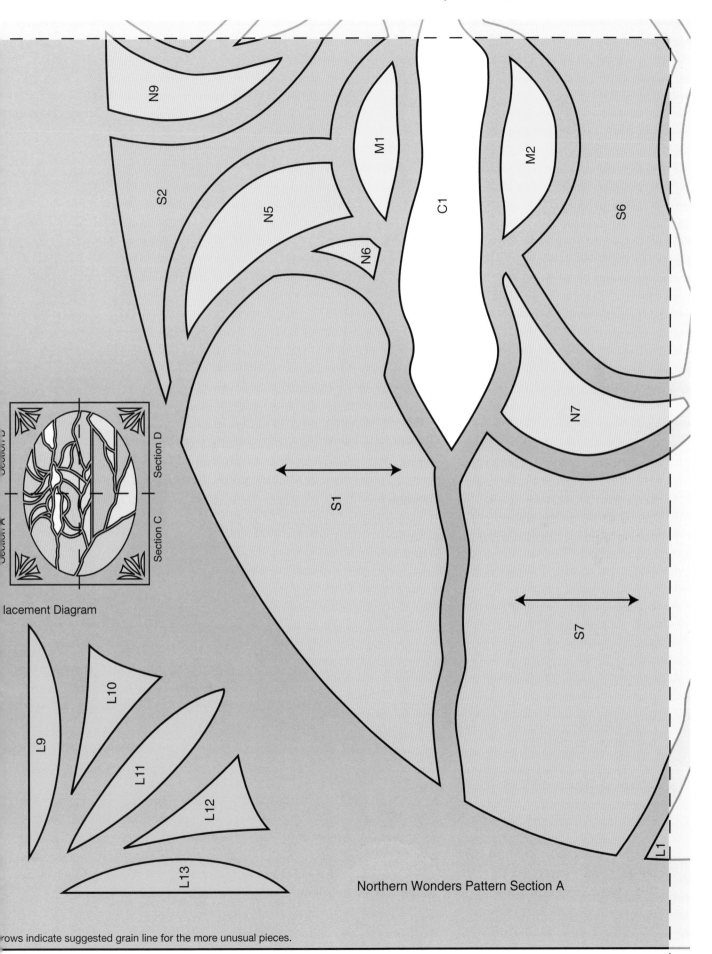

Placement Diagram

Section A
Section B
Section C
Section D

N9

S2

M1

C1

N5

M2

S6

N6

N7

S1

S7

L9

L10

L11

L12

L13

L1

Northern Wonders Pattern Section A

rows indicate suggested grain line for the more unusual pieces.

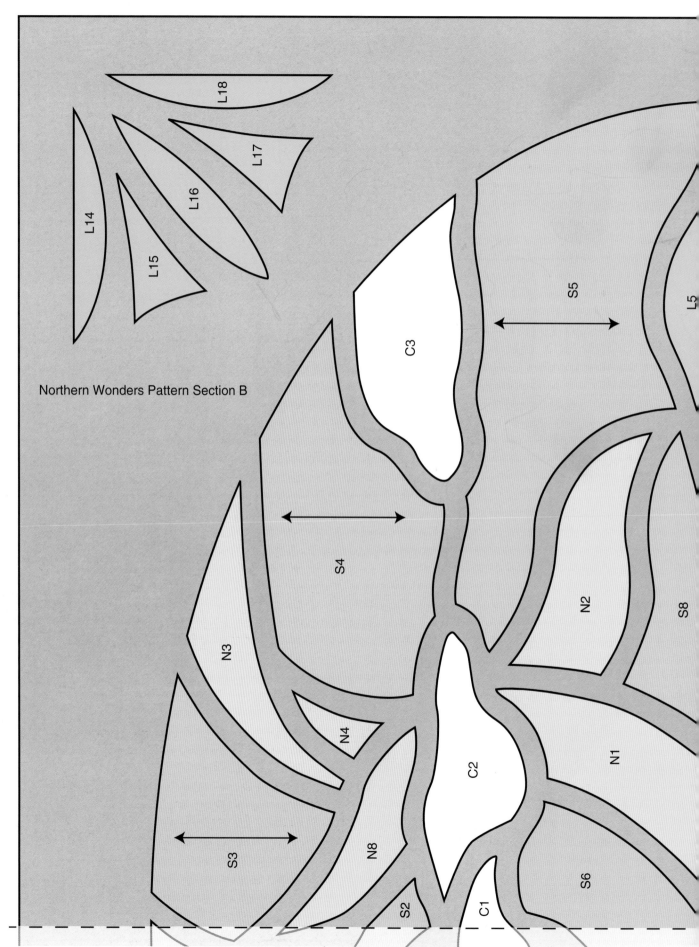

Northern Wonders Pattern Section B

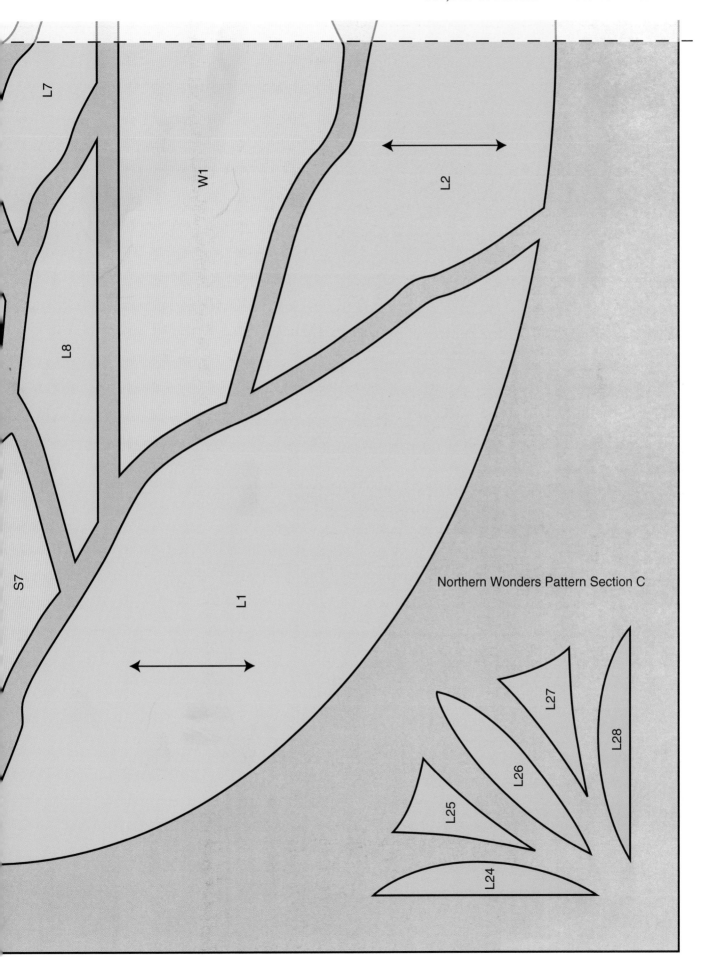

Northern Wonders Pattern Section C

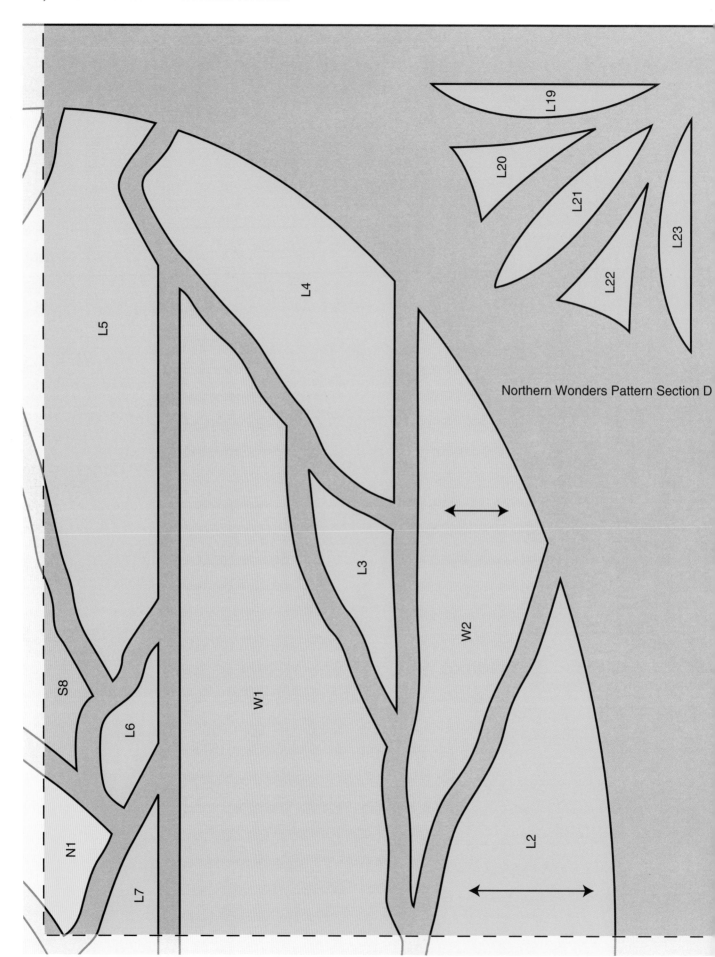

Northern Wonders Pattern Section D

Dancing Blooms

Pattern Size 9½" x 19½" • Quilt Size 13½" x 23½"
Pattern on pages 53–55.

Materials

high-thread-count black fabric for leading, backing, and binding . . . . .1⅛ yd.

background, print gradated on length of grain, pattern S . . . . .⅝ yd.
    or print gradated on cross grain . . . . .½ yd.

small flower, pattern F . . . . .a scrap
large flower, pattern G . . . . .a scrap
leaves, pattern L . . . . .⅛ yd.
border tuck . . . . .⅛ yd.
ultra-thin batting . . . . .½ yd.
fusible transfer web . . . . .½ yd.
poster board, tracing paper, and freezer paper

Create Stained Glass Leading pages 7–9

Page numbers refer to the detailed instructions on Fused Stained Glass Appliqué.

1. The pattern outline for DANCING BLOOMS is 9½" x 19½". Cut a piece of tracing paper about 2" overall larger than your pattern outline. Trace the pattern on pages 53–55 on the tracing paper and secure the tracing to poster board to make a master pattern.
2. Cut a piece of fusible web about 4" overall larger than your pattern outline. Trace the master pattern onto the fusible web backing. Trim the web, leaving ⅜" extra around all four sides of the pattern outline.
3. Cut two 2¼" binding strips from the leading fabric, then unfold the fabric and cut a rectangle on the straight of grain 15" x 25" for the leading lines. Save the remaining fabric for your backing.
4. Fuse the web tracing to the leading fabric. Then cut out the leading lines.

Create Stained Glass Pieces pages 9–11

1. Before making the freezer-paper templates for the stained glass, check to see if any pattern pieces can be combined to reduce the number of templates you will need to cut.
2. Cut a piece of freezer paper about 2" larger overall than your master pattern. Finish making your freezer-paper templates.
3. Cut out your stained glass pieces, leaving the appropriate seam allowances.
4. Audition your stained-glass fabric choices. Then secure the leading to the traced pattern.

Fuse Your Stained Glass pages 11–14

1. To finish your stained glass quilt, start at a bottom corner of the design and position and fuse each piece in place to the back of the leading.
2. Give your stained glass a final check by covering any exposed fusible web and touching up your fused pieces.
3. Trim your quilt top to 13½" x 23½", leaving a 2" border around all sides of the pattern outline. You will be trimming approximately ¾" off each side of your leading fabric.

Finish Your Stained Glass Quilt pages 14–18

To prepare your quilt top for finishing, see the tips and instructions for basting the quilt layers. Secure your fused stained glass pieces by quilting and appliqué stitching all in one, then see the tips for quilting the border. Add the finishing touches by squaring up your quilt, adding a fabric tuck, binding, and signing it.

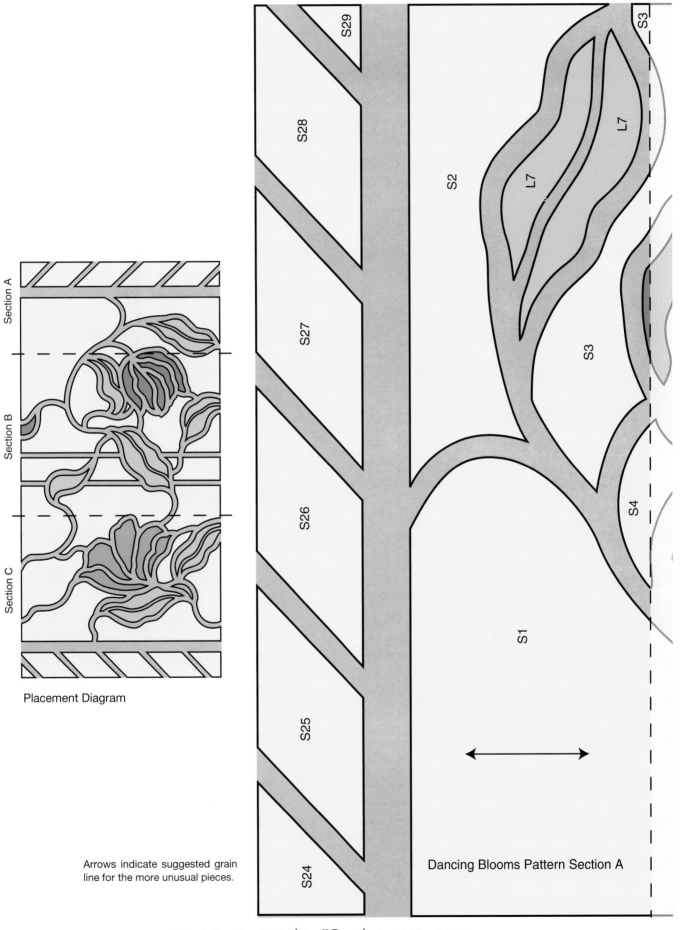

Section A

Section B

Section C

Placement Diagram

Arrows indicate suggested grain line for the more unusual pieces.

S29

S28

S27

S26

S25

S24

S2

L7

L7

L7

S3

S4

S1

S3

Dancing Blooms Pattern Section A

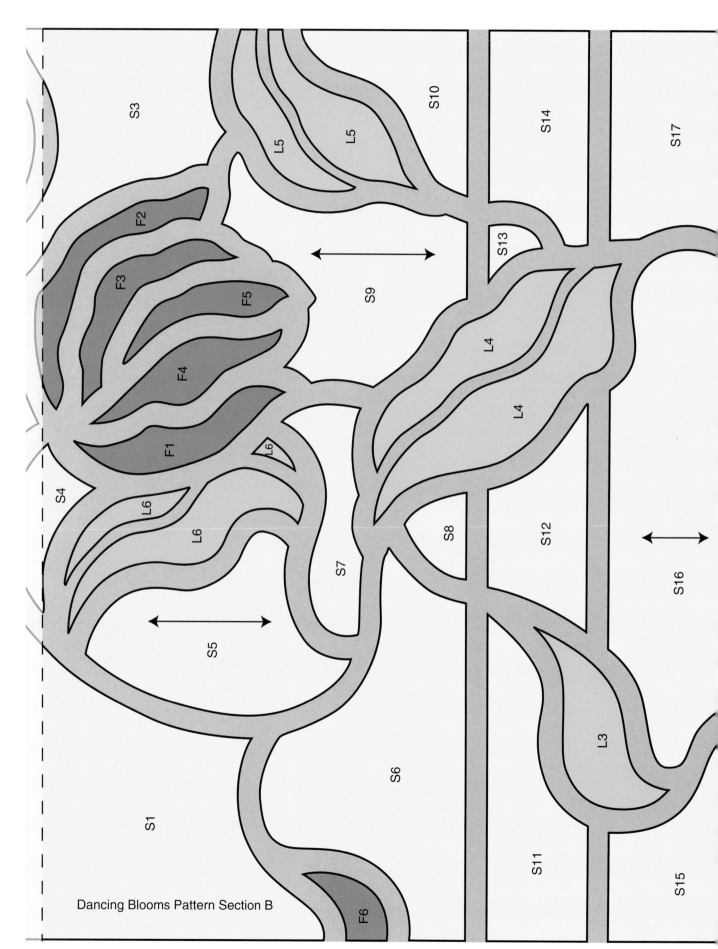

Dancing Blooms Pattern Section B

Dancing Blooms Pattern Section C

Sunrise

Pattern Size 15" x 19" • Quilt Size 17" x 21"
Pattern on pages 58–61.

Materials

high-thread-count black fabric for leading, backing, and binding . . . . .1 yd.
large center suns, pattern S . . . . .¼ yd.
small border suns, pattern A . . . . .⅛ yd.
medium blue, pattern E . . . . .¼ yd.
dark blue, pattern F . . . . .¼ yd.
ultra-thin batting . . . . .⅝ yd.
fusible transfer web . . . . .½ yd.
poster board, tracing paper, and freezer paper

Create Stained Glass Leading pages 7–9

Page numbers refer to the detailed instructions on Fused Stained Glass Appliqué.

1. The pattern outline for SUNRISE is 15" x 19". Cut a piece of tracing paper about 2" overall larger than your pattern outline. Trace the pattern on pages 58–61 on the tracing paper and secure the tracing to poster board to make a master pattern.
2. Cut a piece of fusible web about 4" overall larger than your pattern outline. Trace the master pattern onto the fusible web backing. Trim the web, leaving ⅜" extra around all four sides of the pattern outline.
3. Cut two 2¼" binding strips from the leading fabric, then unfold the fabric and cut a rectangle on the straight of grain 18" x 22" for the leading. Save the remaining fabric for your backing.
4. Fuse the web tracing to the leading fabric. Then cut out the leading lines.

Create Stained Glass Pieces pages 9–11

1. Before making the freezer-paper templates for the stained glass, check to see if any pattern pieces can be combined to reduce the number of templates you will need to cut.
2. Cut a piece of freezer paper about 2" overall larger than your master pattern. Finish making your freezer-paper templates.
3. Cut out your stained glass pieces, leaving the appropriate seam allowances.
4. Audition your stained glass fabric choices. Then secure the leading to the traced pattern.

Fuse Your Stained Glass pages 11–14

1. To finish your stained glass quilt, start at a bottom corner of the design and position and fuse each piece in place to the back of the leading.
2. Give your stained glass a final check by covering any exposed fusible web and touching up your fused pieces.
3. Trim your quilt top to 17" x 21", leaving a 1" border around all sides of the pattern outline. You will be trimming approximately ½" off each side of your leading fabric.

Finish Your Stained Glass Quilt pages 14–18

To prepare your quilt top for finishing, see the tips and instructions for basting the quilt layers. Secure your fused stained glass pieces by quilting and appliqué stitching all in one, then see the tips for quilting the border. Add the finishing touches by squaring up your quilt, binding, and signing it.

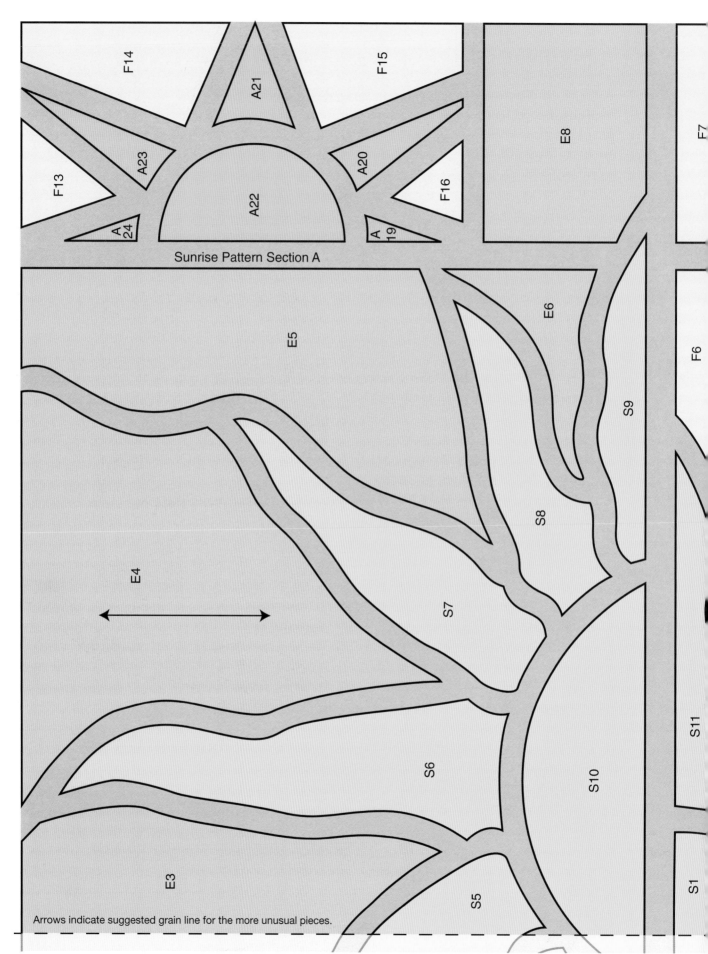

Sunrise Pattern Section A

F14, A21, F15, F13, A23, A22, A20, F16, A24, A19, E8, F7, E5, E6, F6, S9, S8, E4, S7, E3, S6, S10, S5, S11, S1

Arrows indicate suggested grain line for the more unusual pieces.

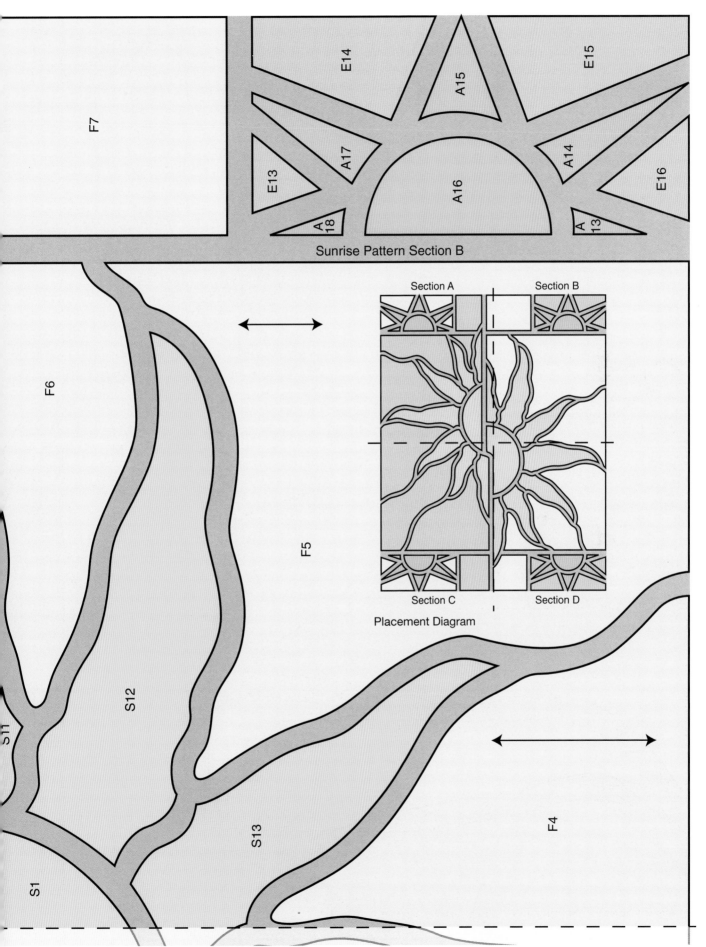

F7

E14

A15

E15

E13

A17

A16

A14

E16

A 18

A 13

Sunrise Pattern Section B

Section A

Section B

F6

F5

S12

S11

S13

S1

F4

Section C

Section D

Placement Diagram

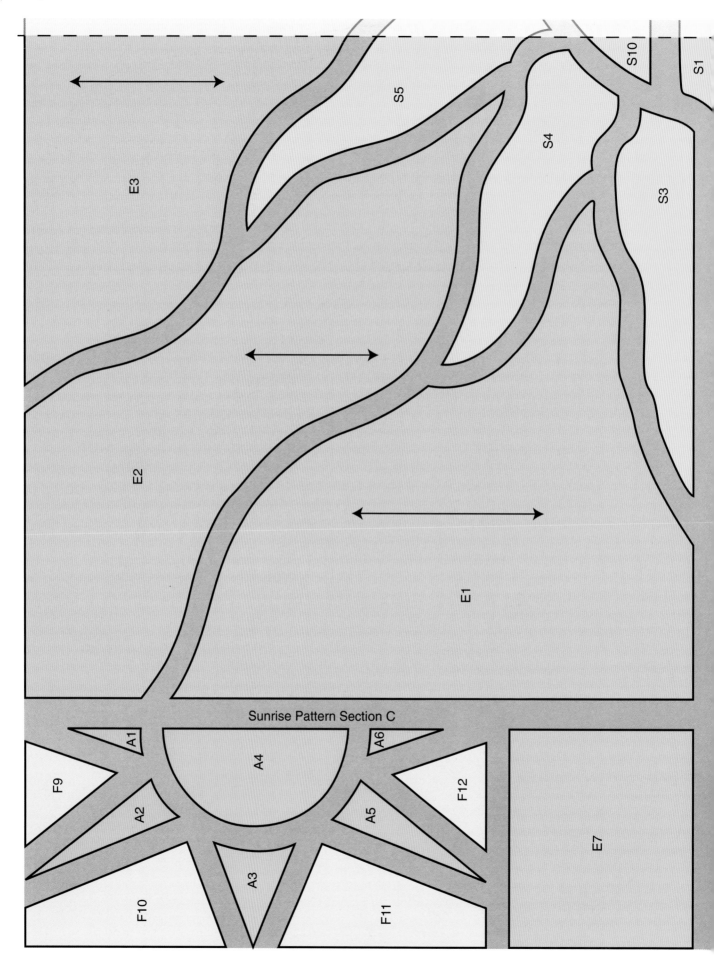

Sunrise Pattern Section C

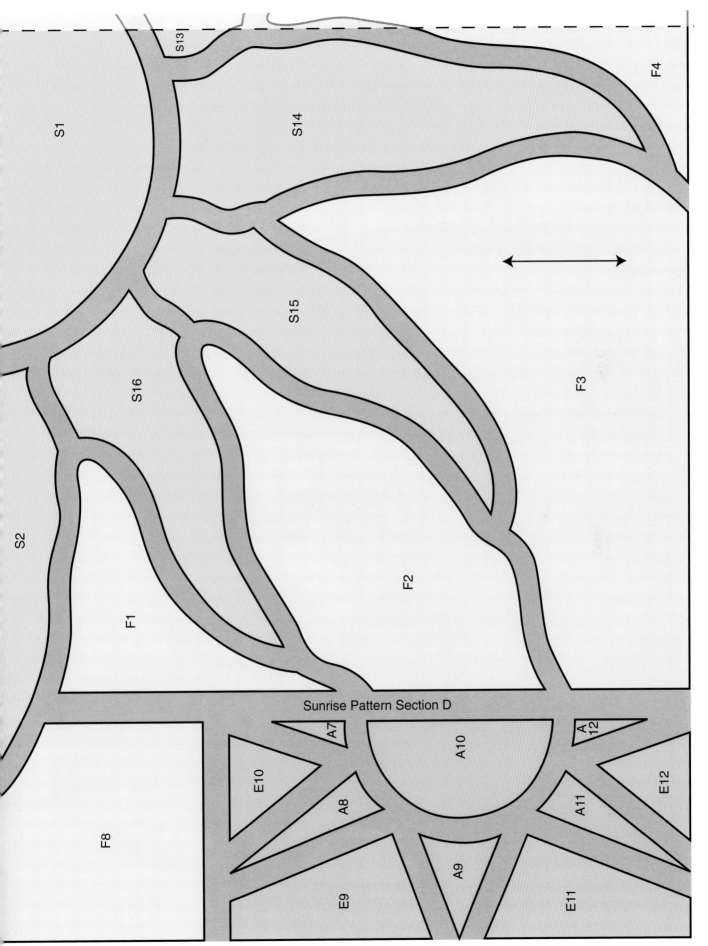

Sunrise Pattern Section D

Singing Soul

Pattern Size 15" x 19⅛" • Quilt Size 19" x 22⅛"
Pattern on pages 64–67.

Materials

high-thread-count black fabric for leading, backing, and binding . . . . .1 yd.
sky, pattern S . . . . .⅓ yd.
grass, pattern G . . . . .¼ yd.
leaves, pattern L . . . . .⅛ each of four different greens
bird's back, pattern M . . . . .⅛ yd.
bird's breast, pattern C . . . . .a scrap or ⅛ yd.
bird's beak, pattern B . . . . .a scrap
bird's throat, pattern T . . . . .a scrap
ultra-thin batting . . . . .⅝ yd.
fusible transfer web . . . . .⅝ yd.
poster board, tracing paper, and freezer paper

Create Stained Glass Leading pages 7–9

Page numbers refer to the detailed instructions on Fused Stained Glass Appliqué.

1. The pattern outline for Singing Soul is 15" x 19⅛". Cut a piece of tracing paper about 2" overall larger than your pattern outline. Trace the pattern on pages 64–67 on the tracing paper and secure the tracing to poster board to make a master pattern.
2. Cut a piece of fusible web about 4" overall larger than your pattern outline. Trace the master pattern onto the fusible web backing. Trim the web, leaving ⅜" extra around all four sides of the pattern outline.
3. Cut two 2¼" binding strips from the leading fabric, then unfold the fabric and cut a rectangle on the straight of grain 20" x 23⅛" for the leading. Save the remaining fabric for your backing.
4. Fuse the web tracing to the leading fabric. Then cut out the leading lines.

Create Stained Glass Pieces pages 9–11

1. The web line that makes the bird's eye is less than ¼" wide. To get a good fuse, trace the two pieces marked M1 as one template and cut it as one piece. Before cutting the freezer-paper templates for the stained glass, check to see if any pattern pieces can be combined to reduce the number of templates you will need to cut.

2. Cut a piece of freezer paper 2" overall larger than your master pattern. Finish making your freezer-paper templates.
3. Cut out your stained glass pieces, leaving the appropriate seam allowances.
4. Audition your stained glass fabric choices. Then secure the leading to the traced pattern.

Fuse Your Stained Glass pages 11–14

1. To finish your stained glass quilt, start at a bottom corner of the design and position and fuse each piece in place to the back of the leading.
2. Give your stained glass a final check by covering any exposed fusible web and touching up your fused pieces.
3. Trim your quilt top to 19" x 22⅛", leaving a 2" border at the top and bottom of the pattern outline and a 1½" on each side of the pattern outline. You will be trimming approximately ½" off each side of your leading fabric.

Finish Your Stained Glass Quilt pages 14–18

To prepare your quilt top for finishing, see the tips and instructions for basting the quilt layers. Secure your fused stained glass pieces by quilting and appliqué stitching all in one, then see the tips for quilting the border. Add the finishing touches by squaring up your quilt, binding, and signing it.

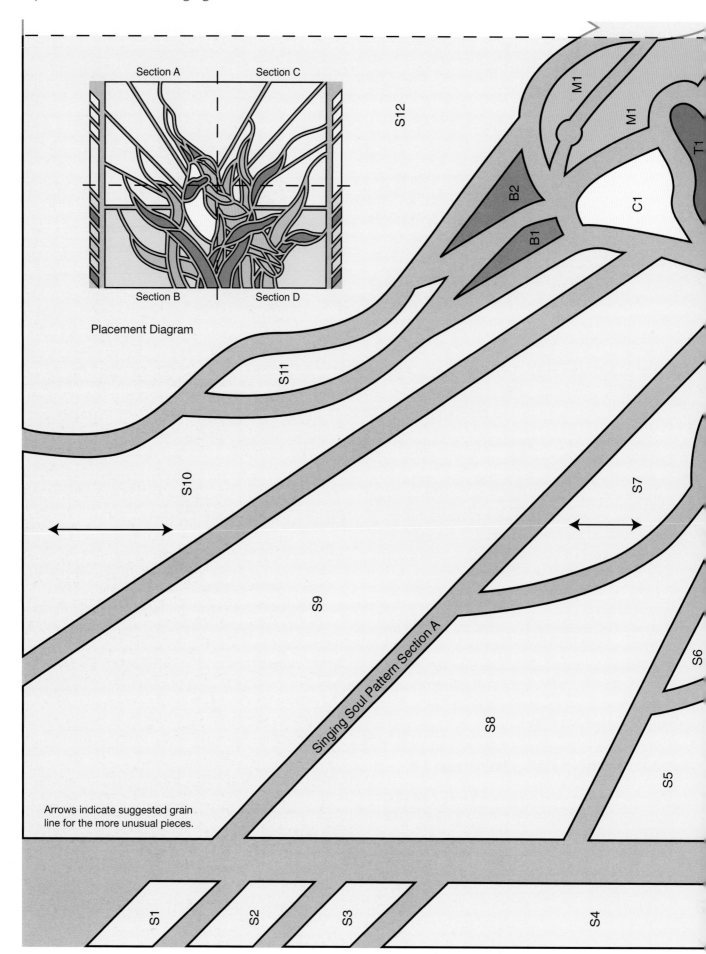

Section A

Section C

Section B

Section D

Placement Diagram

S12

M1

M1

M1

T1

B2

B1

C1

S11

S10

S9

S7

Singing Soul Pattern Section A

S8

S6

S5

S4

S1

S2

S3

Arrows indicate suggested grain
line for the more unusual pieces.

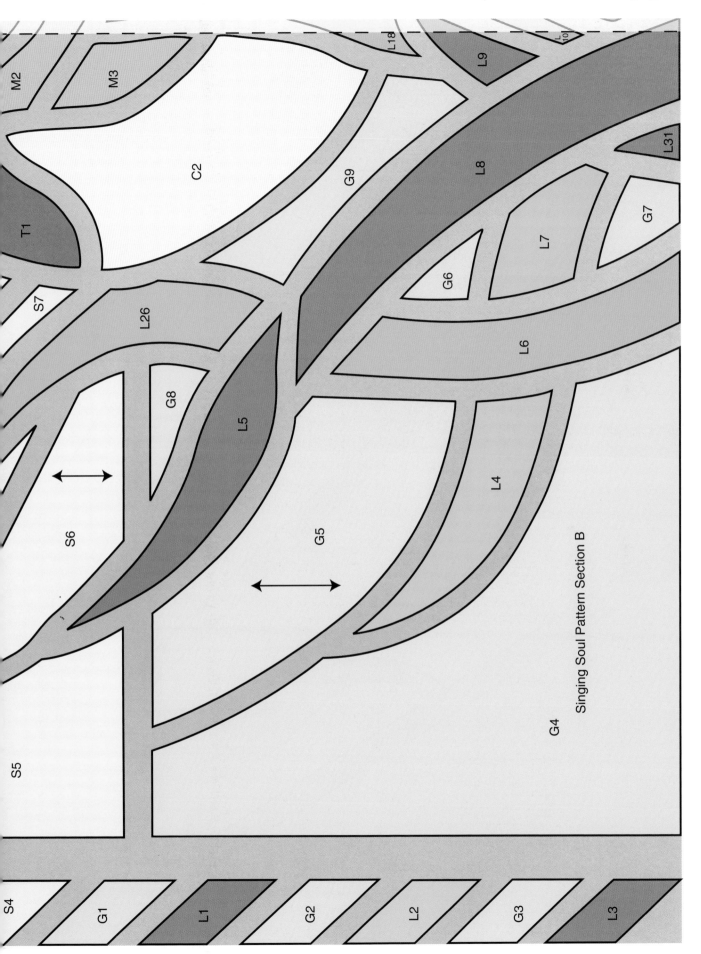

Singing Soul Pattern Section B

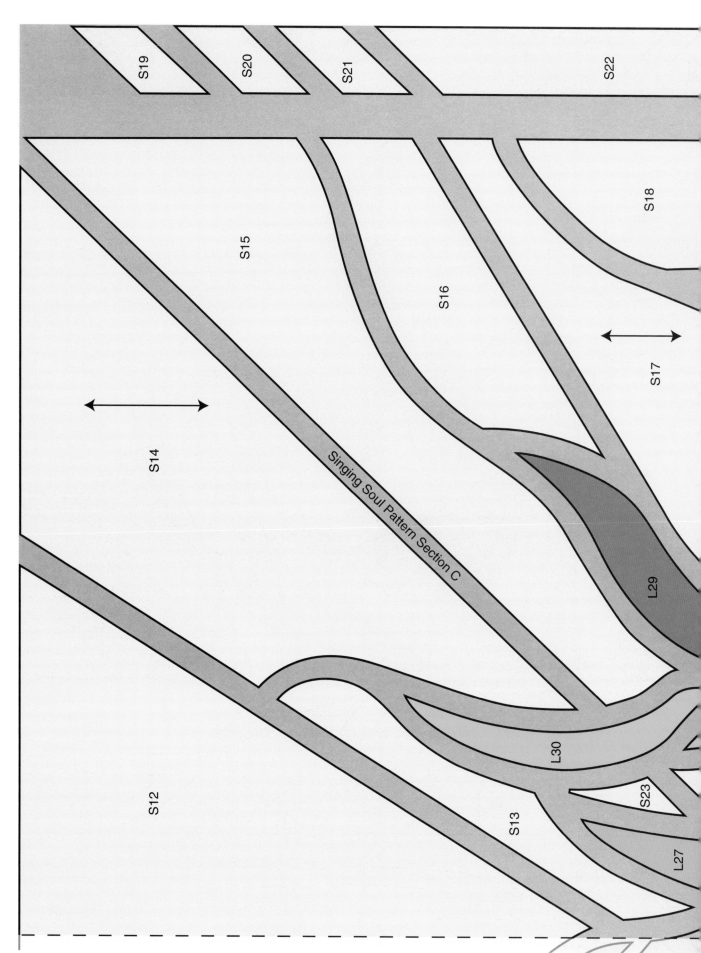

S19

S20

S21

S22

S15

S16

S18

S17

S14

Singing Soul Pattern Section C

L29

S12

L30

S13

S23

L27

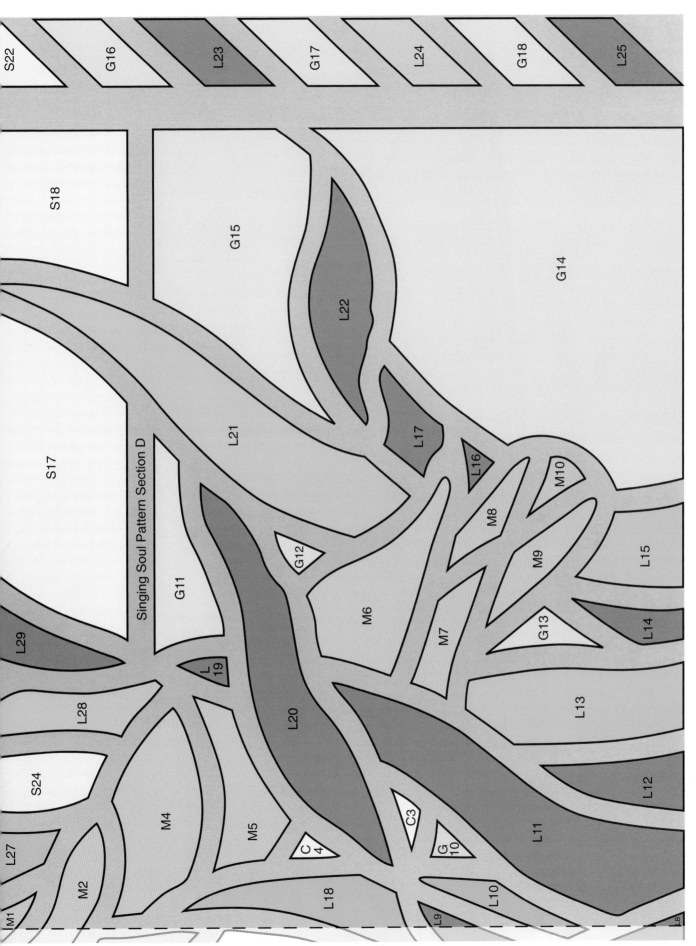

Singing Soul Pattern Section D

Ocean View

Pattern Size 9½" x 22½" • Quilt Size 12½" x 25½"
Pattern on pages 70–72.

Materials

high-thread-count black fabric for leading, backing, and binding . . . . .1 yd.
water, pattern W . . . . .⅓ yd.
purple seaweed, pattern P . . . . .⅛ yd.
green seaweed, pattern S . . . . .⅛ yd.
ocean floor, pattern R . . . . .¼ yd.
fish, pattern F . . . . .⅛ yd.
fish accent, pattern A . . . . .a scrap of yellow
border tuck . . . . .⅛ yd.
ultra-thin batting . . . . .½ yd.
fusible transfer web . . . . .¾ yd.
poster board, tracing paper, and freezer paper

Create Stained Glass Leading pages 7–9

Page numbers refer to the detailed instructions on Fused Stained Glass Appliqué.

1. The pattern outline for OCEAN VIEW is 9½" x 22½". Cut a piece of tracing paper about 2" overall larger than your pattern outline. Trace the pattern on pages 70–72 on the tracing paper and secure the tracing to poster board to make a master pattern.

2. Cut a piece of fusible web about 4" overall larger than your pattern outline. Trace the master pattern onto the fusible web backing. Trim the web, leaving ⅜" extra around all four sides of the pattern outline.

3. Cut two 2¼" binding strips from the leading fabric, then unfold the fabric and cut a rectangle on the straight of grain 14" x 27" for the leading. Save the remaining fabric for your backing.

4. Fuse the web tracing to the leading fabric. Then cut out the leading lines.

Create Stained Glass Pieces pages 9–11

1. The web line in the fish's head is less than ¼" wide. To get a good fuse, trace the two pieces marked F1 as one template and cut it as one piece. Before cutting the freezer-paper templates for the stained glass, check to see if any pattern pieces can be combined to reduce the number of templates you will need to cut.

2. Cut a piece of freezer paper 2" overall larger than your master pattern. Finish making your freezer-paper templates.

3. Cut out your stained glass pieces, leaving the appropriate seam allowances.

4. Audition your stained glass fabric choices. Then secure the leading to the traced pattern.

Fuse Your Stained Glass pages 11–14

1. To finish your stained glass quilt, start at a bottom corner of the design and position and fuse each piece in place to the back of the leading.

2. Give your stained glass a final check by covering any exposed fusible web and touching up your fused pieces.

3. Trim your quilt top to 12½" x 25½", leaving a 1½" border around all sides of the pattern outline. You will be trimming approximately ¾" off each side of your leading fabric.

Finish Your Stained Glass Quilt pages 14–18

To prepare your quilt top for finishing, see the tips and instructions for basting the quilt layers. Secure your fused stained glass pieces by quilting and appliqué stitching all in one, then see the tips for quilting the border. Add the finishing touches by squaring up your quilt, adding a fabric tuck, binding, and signing it.

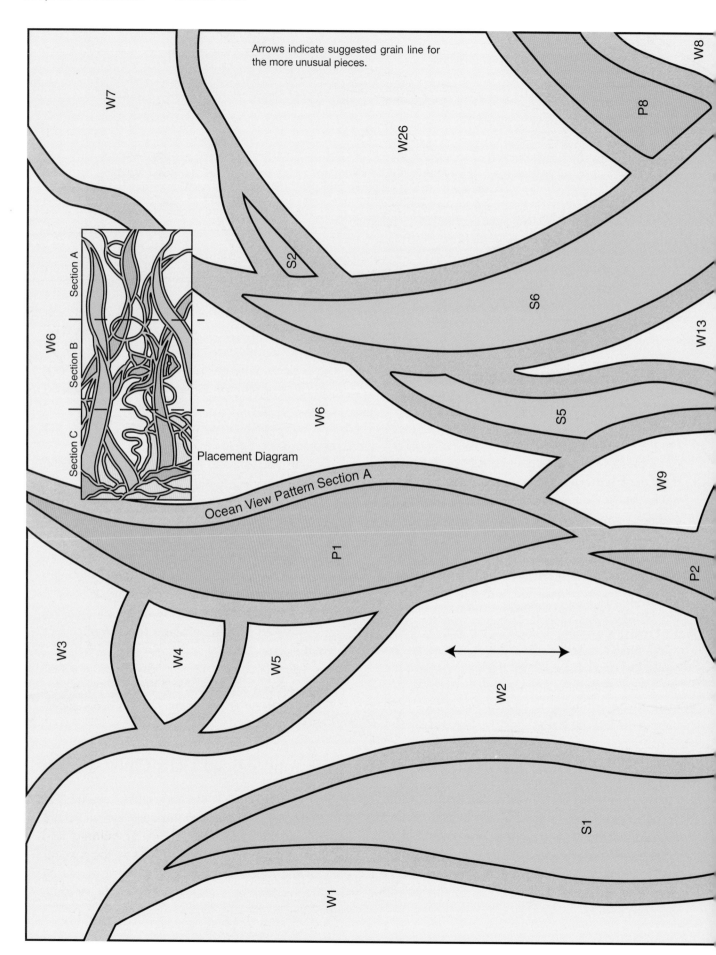

Arrows indicate suggested grain line for the more unusual pieces.

Section A

Section B

Section C

W6

Placement Diagram

Ocean View Pattern Section A

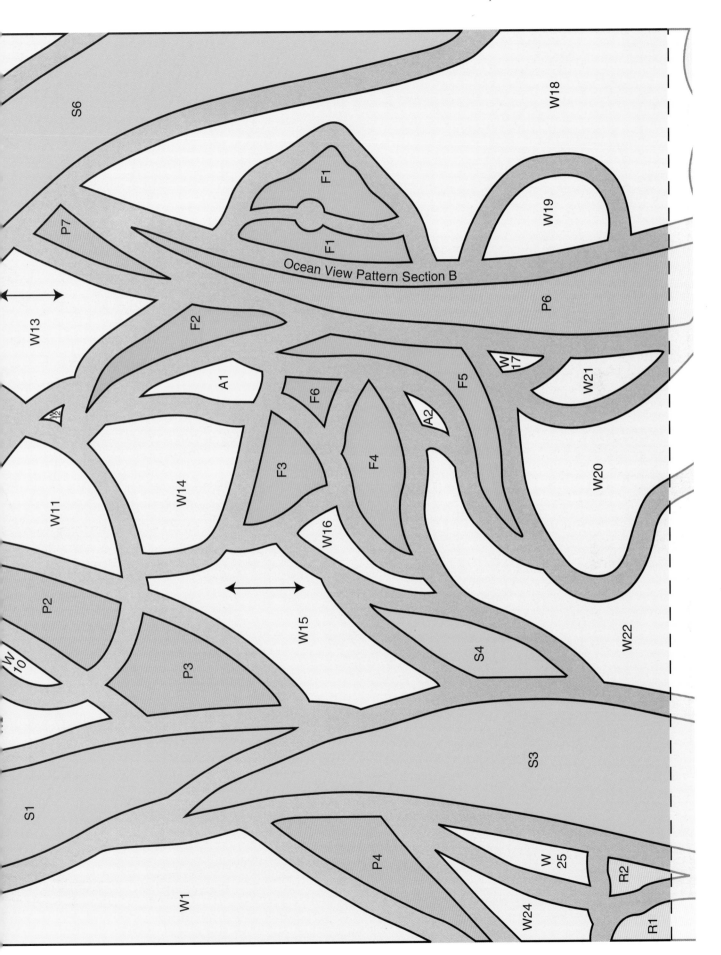

Ocean View Pattern Section B

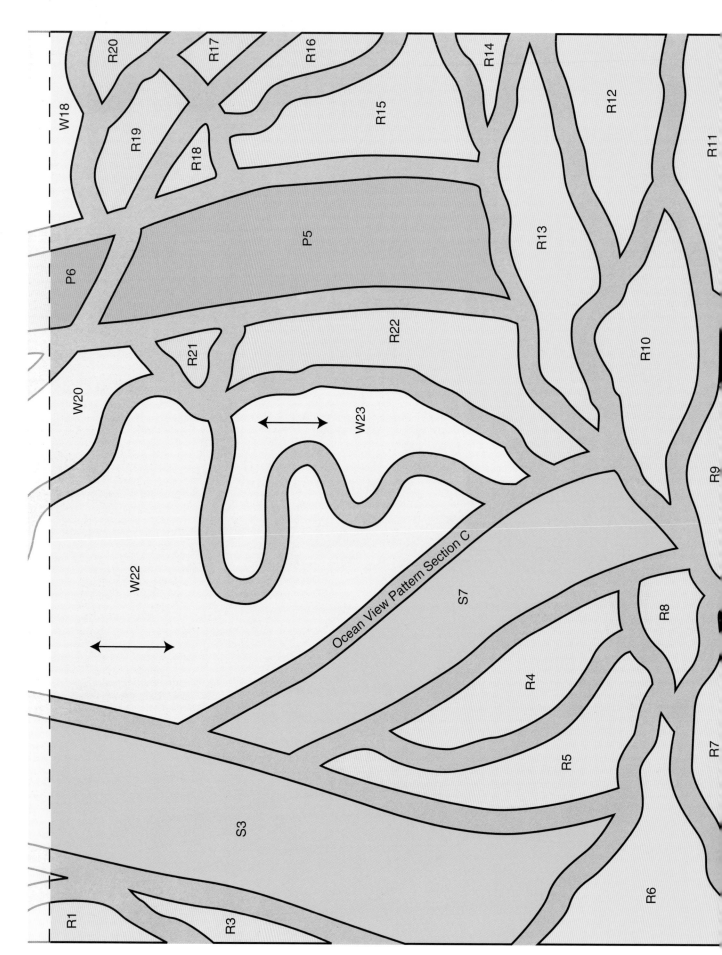

R20
R17
R16
R14
W18
R19
R18
R15
R12
R11
P6
P5
R13
R21
R22
R10
W20
W23
W22
Ocean View Pattern Section C
S7
R9
R4
R8
R5
R7
S3
R6
R1
R3

Pattern Size 15" x 19" • Quilt Size 17½" x 21½"
Pattern on pages 75–78.

Materials

high-thread-count black fabric for leading, backing, and binding . . . . .1 yd.
sunflower petals, pattern S . . . . .¼ yd. of two different yellows
leaves, pattern L . . . . .⅛ yd.
flower center, pattern C . . . . .⅛ yd.
background, pattern B . . . . .⅓ yd.
ultra-thin batting . . . . .½ yd.
fusible transfer web . . . . .⅝ yd.
poster board, tracing paper, and freezer paper

Create Stained Glass Leading pages 7–9

Page numbers refer to the detailed instructions on Fused Stained Glass Appliqué.

1. The pattern outline for SUMMER GLOW is 15" x 19". Cut a piece of tracing paper about 2" overall larger than your pattern outline. Trace the pattern on pages 75–78 on the tracing paper and secure the tracing to poster board to make a master pattern.
2. Cut a piece of fusible web about 4" overall larger than your pattern outline. Trace the master pattern onto the fusible web backing. Trim the web, leaving ⅜" extra around all four sides of the pattern outline.
3. Cut two 2¼" binding strips from the leading fabric, then unfold the fabric and cut a rectangle on the straight of grain 19" x 23" for the leading lines. Save the remaining fabric for your backing.
4. Fuse the web tracing to the leading fabric. Then cut out the leading lines.

Create Stained Glass Pieces pages 9–11

1. Before cutting the freezer-paper templates for the stained glass, check to see if any pattern pieces can be combined to reduce the number of templates you will need to cut.
2. Cut a piece of freezer paper 2" overall larger than your master pattern. Finish making your freezer-paper templates.
3. Cut out your stained glass pieces, leaving the appropriate seam allowances.
4. Audition your stained glass fabric choices. Then secure the leading to the traced pattern.

Fuse Your Stained Glass pages 11–14

1. To finish your stained glass quilt, start at a bottom corner of the design and position and fuse each piece in place to the back of the leading.
2. Give your stained glass a final check by covering any exposed fusible web and touching up your fused pieces.
3. Trim your quilt top to 17½" x 21½", leaving a 1¼" border around all sides of the pattern outline. You will be trimming approximately ¾" off each side of your leading fabric.

Finish Your Stained Glass Quilt pages 14–18

To prepare your quilt top for finishing, see the tips and instructions for basting the quilt layers. Secure your fused stained glass pieces by quilting and appliqué stitching all in one, then see the tips for quilting the border. Add the finishing touches by squaring up your quilt, binding, and signing it.

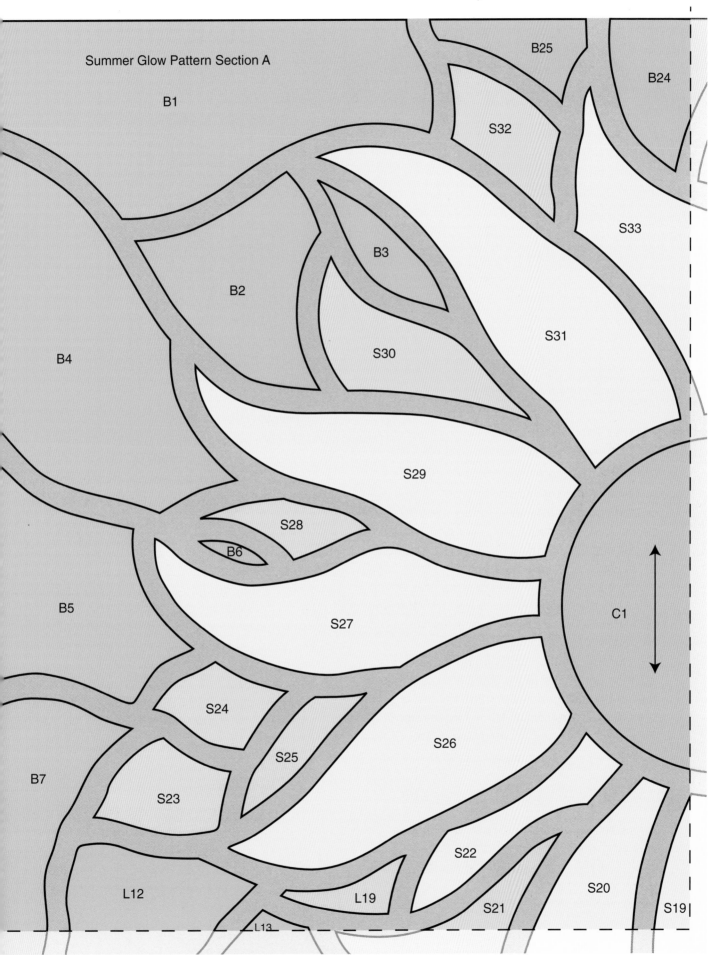

Summer Glow Pattern Section A

B1

B25

B24

S32

B3

S33

B2

S30

S31

B4

S29

S28

B6

S27

B5

C1

S24

S26

B7

S25

S23

S22

S20

L12

L19

S21

S19

L13

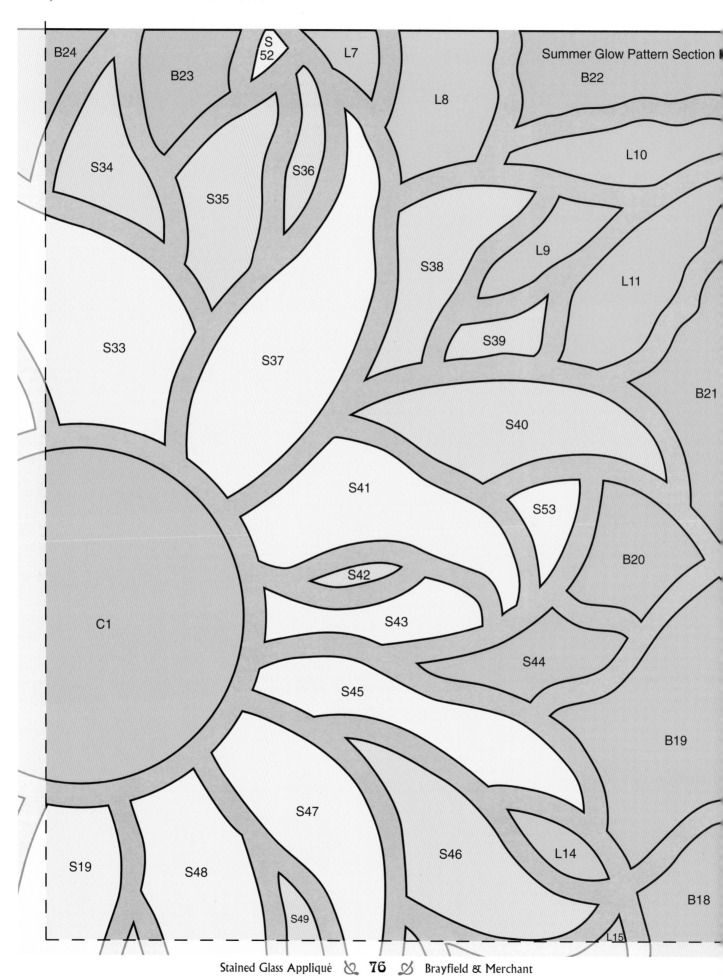

Summer Glow Pattern Section C

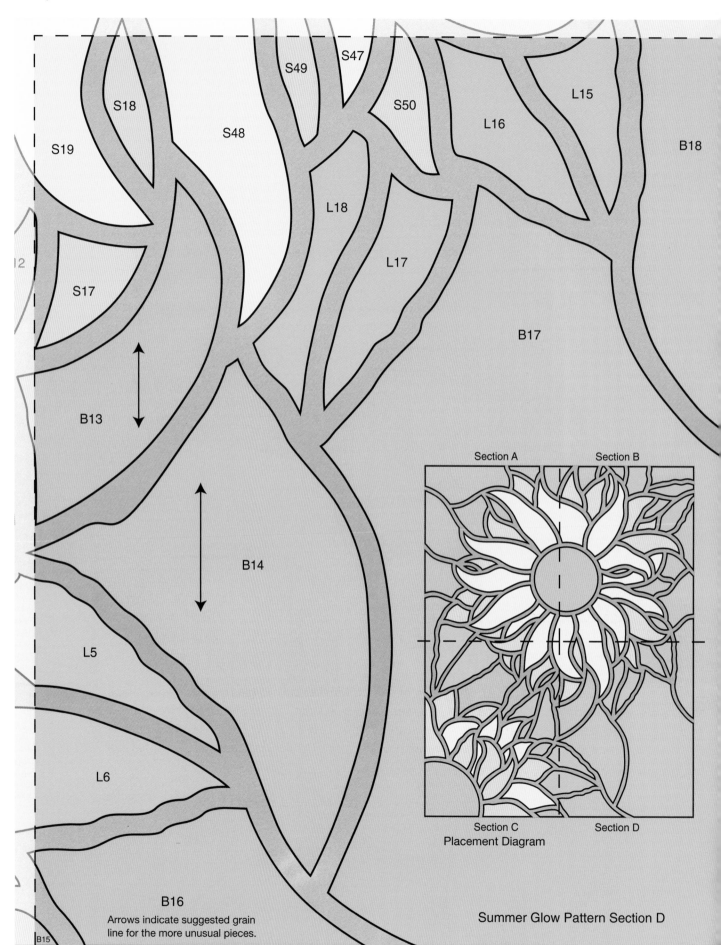

S49

S47

S18

S48

S50

L15

L16

S19

B18

I2

L18

S17

L17

B17

B13

B14

B16

Arrows indicate suggested grain
line for the more unusual pieces.

L5

L6

B15

Section A   Section B

Section C   Section D

Placement Diagram

Summer Glow Pattern Section D

Brenda Brayfield

Born in Northern Ireland, where the fields of the Irish countryside resemble a glorious patchwork quilt, Brenda Brayfield has been playing with fabric for as long as she can remember. Her creative pastimes had always been diverse, but that all changed when she discovered quilting in 1993.

Now, she specializes in modern methods for traditional quilts. As a quiltmaker, teacher, and author, Brenda is well known for her precise methods of quilt construction. In addition to reverse appliqué stained glass, Brenda also creates quilt designs for top foundation piecing, the technique featured in her first book, *Log Cabin Rediscovered by Machine*.

Brenda resides in Surrey, British Columbia, Canada, with her husband, Roger, and their family.

Lise Merchant

Lise Merchant was born in the province of Quebec, Canada, and moved to the Yukon in 1981. An accomplished stained glass artist, Lise has many large commissioned works in government buildings and churches as well as private collections throughout Canada, the United States, and Europe.

The idea of blending her earlier love of sewing with her stained glass designs took shape when she mentioned the idea to a friend and quilt shop owner. She discovered that the two passions blend and complement each other very well. Quilting occupies most of Lise's time now. She has her own pattern line called Seams Like Glass Designs available at www.seamslikeglass.com.

Lise lives in Whitehorse, Yukon, with her husband, Philip, and their children.

Other AQS Books

This is only a small selection of the books available from the American Quilter's Society. AQS books are known worldwide for timely topics, clear writing, beautiful color photos, and accurate illustrations and patterns. The following books are available from your local bookseller, quilt shop, or public library.

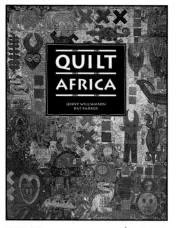

#6510   us$21.95

#5761   us$22.95

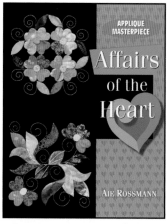

#6517   us$21.95

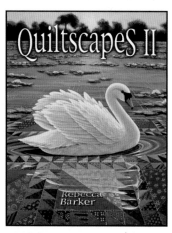

#6680   us$21.95

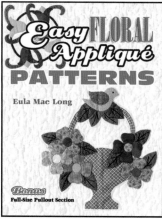

#6300   us$24.95

#6295   us$24.95

#6407   us$21.95

#6511   us$22.95

#5234   us$22.95

LOOK for these books nationally. CALL **1-800-626-5420**
or VISIT our Web site at **www.americanquilter.com**